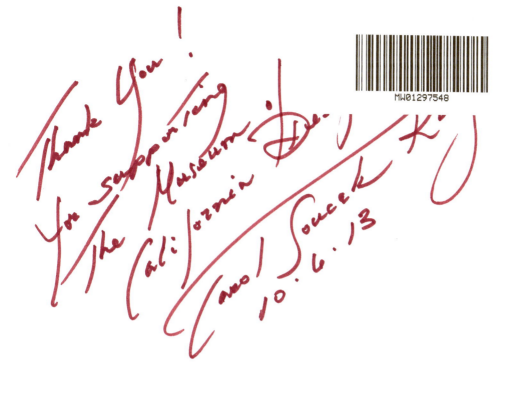

Thank You!
For supporting
The Museum of
California Design
Carol Soucek K
10.6.13

When I was 12-years-old,

I envisioned that I would write

a book like this as I neared 70.

[Springtime 2012]

Under the Bridges at Arroyo del Rey

The Salon on the Spiritually Creative Life

Carol Soucek King

Illustrated by Miller Yee Fong

UNDER THE BRIDGES AT ARROYO DEL REY
The Salon on the Spiritually Creative Life

Copyright © 2012 by Carol Soucek King

All rights reserved. No part of this book may be used or reproduced in any manner whatsoever without written permission except in the case of brief quotations embodied in critical articles and reviews. For information contact the publisher.

Published by:
Carol Soucek King and Richard King Center for Architecture, Arts and the Humanities
60 El Circulo Drive, Pasadena, California 91105

Available through:
www.createspace.com/4025479
www.amazon.com and other retailers

Illustrations by Miller Yee Fong
Graphic Design by Bryan Bosworth / BBcreative

Library of Congress Cataloguing-in-Publication Data
King, Carol Soucek.

UNDER THE BRIDGES AT ARROYO DEL REY
The Salon on the Spiritually Creative Life

Carol Soucek King – First Edition

Inspirational, Creativity, Spirituality, Salon Gatherings,
Architecture/Art/Landscape - Psychological Aspects

ISBN-13:9781480101005 (softcover)
ISBN-10:1480101001 (softcover)
LCCN:2012919423

Printed in North Charleston, South Carolina

To Richard and all the others

with whom I have been privileged

to share this blessed life.

CONTENTS

PRELUDE	7
TALE I Our Home STABILITY	8
TALE II In the Garden GROWTH	36
TALE III At the Water's Edge POSSIBILITY	52
TALE IV Maintaining the Grounds HUMOR	68
TALE V Building Bridges UNDERSTANDING	84
TALE VI Our *Real* Estate KINDNESS	102
TALE VII Pavilions of the Mind HARMONY	118
TALE VIII The Creek Never Ends LOVE	138
TALE IX Empowered Places HEALING	154
TALE X Sanctuary SPIRITUALITY	170
AFTERWORD	189
CREATE YOUR OWN SALON	190
ACKNOWLEDGMENTS	193
ABOUT THE AUTHOR AND ILLUSTRATOR/BOOK DESIGNER	196

Native Americans crossing the Arroyo, circa 1730

PRELUDE

PROVIDING A LEGACY

by Richard King, HonDB

THE SALON ON THE SPIRITUALLY CREATIVE LIFE, MAY 2010

REMARKS

My love affair with the Arroyo Seco, so named by the Spaniards when they arrived here hundreds of years ago during an unusually dry period, started in 1978 when our two acres of land found my wife and me. To us, it is like no other place on the face of the earth. The memories of Indians, Spanish explorers, orange groves and ostriches – yes, there was an ostrich farm here! – make this a very special place – a sanctuary, a retreat, a flow of endless energy and spirituality. I never want it to end, and it won't. Several years ago Carol and I decided that, when our spirits move on, our house with its surrounding gardens, designed by architects Conrad Buff III and Don Hensman in 1979, will be given to the University of Southern California's School of Architecture. It will become the Carol Soucek King and Richard King Center for Architecture, Arts and the Humanities in perpetuity. So we will join the Native Americans, Spaniards and orange growers – proud that we have provided a legacy for the "dry" creek.

TALE 1 Our Home
STABILITY

Love is everything.
Without Love there is nothing.
Express Love toward everyone
with whom our lives we share,
Toward every creature,
every place entrusted to our care.

Love elevates what we do.
Love illuminates what we say.
No matter how big,
No matter how small,
Life's every aspect
Love makes worthwhile.

Love is everything.
Without Love there is nothing.
Express Love toward everyone
with whom our lives we share,
Toward every creature,
every place entrusted to our care.

The majestic 1913 Colorado Street Bridge,
Arroyo Seco south of Arroyo del Rey

OUR HOME - STABILITY

Richard and I were both gypsies, in a way, when we went searching for the property on which to build our home. Neither of us had many possessions, most having been left behind in earlier parts of our lives. But we knew what we wanted ... a sense of seclusion, a sense of being hidden away in nature ... and a place more rustic and wild than urban and manicured. And we knew we wanted a home and garden that could be maintained easily within our financial and physical ability, so that they might be never a burden but a joy. And more than anything, we wanted it to be welcoming to our own spiritual leanings and those of others. We were already envisioning the type of meaningful gatherings that The Salon on the Spiritually Creative Life would prove to be.

Conrad Buff III, FAIA, and Donald C. Hensman, FAIA, had become our most admired architects. During the first year we were married, we fell in love with the rigorous earthy simplicity of their post-and-beam Mid-20th-Century Modernist homes. A year later, we asked them if they might consider creating a home for us. All we wanted was a small house, we told them. The main thing was that it should be a serene haven in the midst of nature, so that both house and garden could serve our lifestyles of writing, reading, meeting with students and associates and pursuing other creative interests. Conrad and Don said "yes," and soon after we started looking for land on which to build.

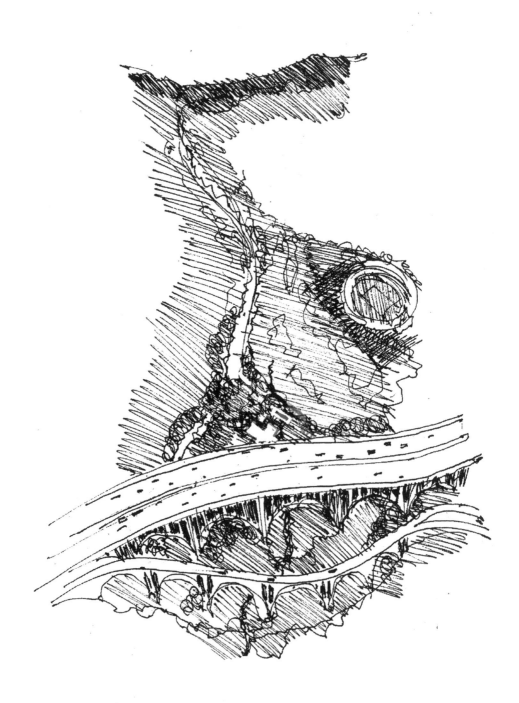

Aerial view of Arroyo del Rey, bounded on the South by the 134 Freeway and Colorado Street bridges and bounded on the North by the Rose Bowl and Brookside Golf Course.

Even in 1978 available land in Pasadena, California, was scarce and whatever did exist was reputed to be financially out-of-sight. Yet one day when we were bemoaning our lack of success in finding property suitable for our goal – a site of uncultivated wilderness flat enough to accommodate the simple, serenely horizontal and small dwelling we envisioned – Conrad and Don mentioned one possibility. It was a two-acre parcel in Pasadena's Arroyo Seco that most people assumed to be part of the surrounding public park. Yet Conrad and Don knew it was privately owned and had previously suggested it to clients. One by one, however, all had felt it too unusual for their tastes.

The reason? The property was situated just north of the 134 freeway that soars high above from east to west. But to Conrad and Don, that freeway bridge, with its giant concrete arches that echo those of the historic Colorado Street Bridge which is visible a little farther south, provided a dramatic yet protective backdrop to the land below. The view north revealed yet another similarly graceful structure – the Holly Street Bridge with a view of the San Gabriel Mountains beyond. As described by Pasadena Heritage, the bridges were carefully designed "not solely to move vehicles over the Arroyo but to create something picturesque for the community."

The moment Richard and I walked out under that freeway bridge and onto the land, encircled by old walls of river rock and California live oaks and with a meandering creek marking its perimeter to the north and east, we felt it was ours. And we were lucky. When Richard, Don and Conrad tracked down the man who had owned the land for ages, he was living in northern California, was surprised to learn that he still owned the property and accepted our first offer.

Howard and Tom Oshiyama overlooking the pool, their gaze directed north toward the Arroyo, the Holly Street Bridge, and the San Gabriel Mountains

Before long Conrad and Don had designed and built the main house and pool, using a minimum of materials and space to suit our requirement for affordability, easy care and to live lightly on the land. Six years later they designed in the same spirit the Pavilion (our studio/guest house) and tennis court, and later still, after Conrad had passed away, Don designed the Gazebo down by the creek. To connect all three structures as well as provide a seemingly endless invitation for wandering, they worked along with landscape contractors Howard

Oshiyama and his son Tom with whom they had a long relationship of trust based on their similar reverence for nature. Paths of river rock, large stepping stones and railroad ties lead through an abundant array – oleander bushes, eucalyptus, podocarpus, bamboo, oak and acacia trees, azaleas, agapanthus plants and naturally worn boulders ideal for sitting. All provide sequestered opportunities to rest, contemplate, then start out again.

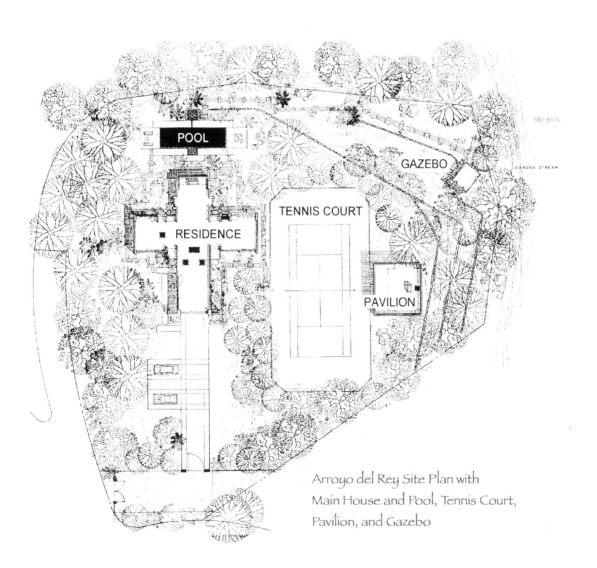

Arroyo del Rey Site Plan with Main House and Pool, Tennis Court, Pavilion, and Gazebo

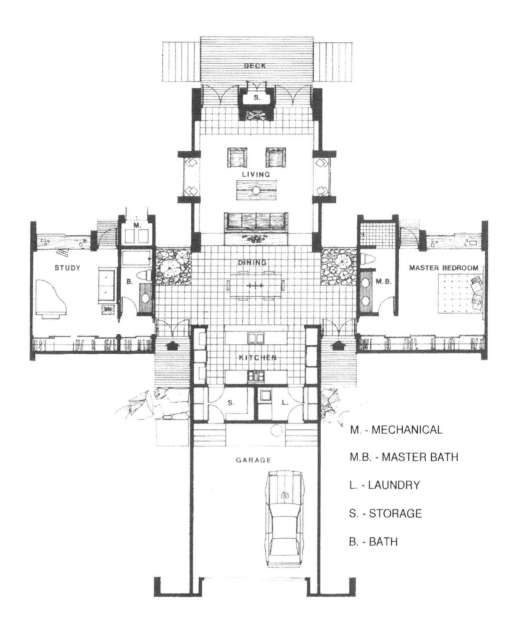

Arroyo del Rey
Main House Floor Plan

"In a garden as in life, you don't want to see everything at once," they would explain. "You want to feel there is always something more beyond."

Conrad and Don continued that metaphor for living in the design of the house itself. The plan, with one large living/dining/kitchen area balanced on both sides by an equally-sized room and bath [one the master suite, the other an office], is straightforward. Yet by placing the front entry off-center of the main living area, and by their masterful manipulation of proportion and contrast, the architects introduced into all that simplicity a sense of surprise that continues throughout. The slight changes in floor levels add to the vitality of this experience. A sense of open space is enhanced by large windows and glass for all perimeter doors and also by the built-in furnishings, designed by the architects to be integral to the structure's specific dimensions.

Every detail is treated like precious jewelry – from the stained glass doors by artist Judy Jansen, to the teak cabinetry, to the coffee table and bathroom fittings crafted and finished by Conrad himself. Even the gigantic boulders, found on the property and personally placed by Conrad and Don as the steps at each entry, were treated as gems.

The resulting effect is a feeling of total perfection, which was their genius. And that is the reason that I, having written many books about some of the most coveted residences in the world, have never wished to live anyplace else than at Arroyo del Rey - the name suggested by Conrad's wife Libby and which means "Creek of the King."

Don Hensman and contractors celebrate
the completion of the Gazebo, 1993

What Conrad and Don had given us was a part of their contribution to what has come to be known as the USC Style because of the University of Southern California's impact on mid-twentieth-century architecture. But perhaps the greatest part of Conrad and Don's gift to us was the sense of harmony with which they listened to our dreams and carried them forth, not only through their graceful design but also through their attitude and the attitude that they insisted that others express. It was a great lesson, and one they emphasized repeatedly over the following years as we completed each stage of development. Even when he completed the Gazebo, Don planned a small Japanese luncheon on its open redwood floor to honor the Oshiyamas, Buff & Hensman associate architect Dennis Smith whom Don later made a partner in the firm, and also the seismic consultant, the carpenters and the stonemasons.

Throughout their work, Don and Conrad were quietly saluting the qualities of peacefulness and civility that they knew were more important than the architecture itself. Indeed, the pervading sense of these architects' gentility has made an indelible mark on Arroyo del Rey and is felt by all those who gather for The Salon on the Spiritually Creative Life.

THE CREATIVE SPACE BETWEEN THEORY AND PRACTICE

Scott Johnson, FAIA

THE SALON ON THE SPIRITUALLY CREATIVE LIFE, MARCH 2010

"It's a delight to be in this extraordinary house," said architect Scott Johnson, partner-in-charge of Johnson Fain Partners and author of two books discussing the relationship in architecture between theory and practice. "I have heard about this place that Buff & Hensman created for the Kings, but I've not previously been here. It's a perfect house.

"For some reasons in many cultures, there is a separation between the world of theory and ideas and the world of making things. And the offspring of that sort of thinking are things like 'well, the art world is crap.' Even in the university where I have spent some time, there is the thought that, if you think, if you're part of the world of ideas, then maybe you're not really that good at making things. And if you're ever over here making things, you're probably not that deep in your thinking. And I thought, 'That's an unfortunate separation.

And in architecture, it's particularly unfortunate. Because we're trying to use our hands and our hearts and our minds, trying to make something that resonates on all levels.'

Scott Johnson's Salon in the King Living Room

"In architecture in particular, and also in science and engineering, there's the idea that thinking and ideas don't really matter, that we're just on this march to the sea, and that some of our most famous current architects don't make reference to theory. But in reality, buildings are based on a whole set of ideas. And in both of my books exploring the validity of this concept, *The Great Idea* and *Tall Building*, I found again and again that the making of a building resonates with all kinds of different ideas, that making stuff is not divorced from ideas."

Arroyo del Rey demonstrates this, as Scott Johnson said, in a way that is "perfect." Conrad and Don melded their own impassioned ideas with ours so that our home could truly serve Richard and me as center of our universe. As international business consultant, university trustee, community leader, educator, and author, Richard is ever letting new ideas evolve within the context of our own home. He brings its rooms and gardens alive with visitors from other lands as he continues his lifelong devotion to building bridges between world cultures, especially between the United States and Asia. For myself, after spending many decades at my offices which were located elsewhere, our home has become the center of all of my activities. It is here where I write my books and where in 1996 I started The Salon on the Spiritually Creative Life.

The result of letting our home serve as a center for our activities is that there is little distinction between our professional, social and personal lives. This sense of all-inclusiveness between work and play has made evident to us that the process of creativity is as nurturing as the final creation.

THE FREEMAN HOUSE: TALE OF A FRANK LLOYD WRIGHT MASTERPIECE

Kenneth Alan Breisch, Ph D

Founder, Programs in Historic Preservation,
School of Architecture, University of Southern California

THE SALON ON THE SPIRITUALLY CREATIVE LIFE, SEPTEMBER 2009

One person who has understood that the process of creating a home is as much the goal as is the "finished" home itself is Ken Breisch, architectural historian and founder of the USC School of Architecture's

Graduate Programs in Historic Preservation. Years ago, when The Gamble House by architects Greene & Greene was given to the university, it was in good condition and ready for tours and study. Yet that was not the case when USC was given another historic architectural treasure, the Freeman House by Frank Lloyd Wright.

As Ken Breisch related: "Wright designed The Freeman House for Harriet and Samuel Freeman in late 1923 and completed it in early 1925. It is a masterpiece by one of the world's greatest architects, so when Harriet Freeman willed it to the University of Southern California's School of Architecture, this was an immense gift. However its physical condition was far short of perfection – a state that many would have considered a liability.

"Yet shortly before her death two years later, Mrs. Freeman penned a few lines that described her vision for the house that were simple and direct. The Freeman House, she wrote, was to be a practical house for work – for educational, productive work by students and teachers and everyone interested in this great architect, Frank Lloyd Wright. All the house needs, she said, is what is necessary for it to be made efficient – it need not be a house rebuilt to its original perfection for it to be of service.

"In light of Mrs. Freeman's wishes, the school has been using the residence as a research laboratory, a place for students to engage in dis-

The Freeman House, 1925, by Frank Lloyd Wright

cussions concerning the future of the house. They have been carefully studying the composition of the concrete block system that Wright used to construct it, and have debated its significance in the career of the architect and within the cultural history of Los Angeles and Hollywood. While occasionally open to the public, its primary function for the forseeable future will be - in line with the wishes of the woman who commissioned it and occupied it for more than sixty years - as a place for students and teachers to work and study.

"Unlike the school's other historical showplace, Greene and Greene's Gamble House, and what will likely be the physical condition of Richard and Carol King's Arroyo del Rey when it becomes USC's property, the Freeman House was in a state of severe disrepair. Yet Mrs. Freeman saw this not as a negative but as a positive - and we at USC have, too. The process itself is the destination."

Detail of FLW textile block at the Freeman House

Serendipity ruled supreme with the bequeathing to USC of three architectural treasures that are linked by their commonalities, despite the seventy-year span between the first and last of their completion dates. They are Greene & Greene's 1908 Gamble House, Frank Lloyd Wright's 1925 Freeman House and now our home, Buff & Hensman's 1979 King Residence. All are distinguished by an abiding respect for the site, response to the hospitable Southern California climate, the use of natural native materials, a deft sense of proportion, dramatic variations in scale, and attention to handcrafted details inside and out. Of particular note is that these architects not only designed these details but also in many cases personally fabricated them. Moreover, each home gives individual expression to each client's idea of a structure that would provide a sense of the stability of a strong home base.

More similarities are ready to be discovered, as comparisons are easily accessible. All three homes are located a short distance between each other and from the University of Southern California itself.

Coffee table designed and crafted by Conrad Buff III in the King Living Room

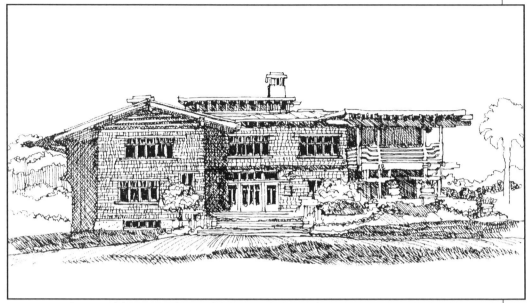

The Gamble House by architects Greene and Greene, 1908

Shade and shadow on the back porch of the Gamble House

Lantern on the clinker brick wall at the Gamble House

As did Mrs. Freeman and as USC continues to do today, my husband Richard has always emphasized that the process is just as important as the destination. That perspective has greatly influenced our thinking as he and I have walked these grounds at Arroyo del Rey, wondering who might have walked this land before us. For example, we have questioned the origin of Arroyo del Rey's encircling stone walls – who built them and why? Richard hoped that they might have been built for some worthy purpose, a purpose that might have truly helped the area's earlier dwellers rather than be merely ornamental, but none of the historians we had as yet consulted could ascribe the walls' origin with any certitude.

Also, the concept of equating process with destination has always been influential in our pondering the future of Arroyo del Rey and who might use it after we have ceased navigating its winding paths. For many years, we hoped that the people who came after us will preserve our home and gardens and continue to open them to the community as we have done. For that reason, it has been one of our lives' greatest privileges to have the University of Southern California agree to preserve Arroyo del Rey for future generations to use, enjoy and study.

Then, at one Salon [pages 29-33], we learned that the stone walls and even the idea of this property serving the community had their genesis more than one hundred years earlier.

'LET ME WALK IN BEAUTY': LANDSCAPE, NATURE AND SPIRITUALITY AT THE KING HOUSE

Heather Goers, Architectural Historian

THE SALON ON THE SPIRITUALLY CREATIVE LIFE, SEPTEMBER 2011

It was at this salon that many of the intimations that Richard and I had about this land were given historical context. From our first walk onto its vast flat plateau above the creek, and later when we were designing our home and garden with architects Conrad Buff III and Don Hensman and landscape contractor Howard Oshiyama, we felt surrounded by a kind and harmonious sensibility. We assumed it came from the centuries of earlier peoples dwelling peacefully here. And that was surely part of it. Yet, when we learned there was something even more concrete, Richard and I welcomed the news as positive affirmation of how we ourselves have viewed this property's treasure and what we have decided for its future.

Heather Goers, a Master's candidate in Historic Preservation at the University of Southern California, reported that she had unearthed

Scoville Barn on the west bank of the Arroyo Seco, 1888
– now part of the Kings' property

documentation that in 1886 real estate developer/businessman James W. Scoville had purchased the property that is now ours. At the time, the land was thought to have little value because it was completely undeveloped – steep and overgrown with an almost impenetrable underbrush, and filled with wild animals. Scoville, however, saw the potential of the land and made plans to transform the area into a park – one that would be privately owned, yet open to the public.

"A lifelong philanthropist as well as a successful businessman, James Scoville strongly believed in helping those less fortunate, and his plans for a park provided the means to do just that. The property required a great deal of preparation before anything could be built, so Scoville hired local men who had lost their jobs in Pasadena's recent economic downturn and put them to work clearing and grading the land. Over the next several years Scoville's workers created many features that were as useful to the Pasadenans as they were beautiful, including terraced stone retaining walls, graded roads and the first public bridge connecting the east and west banks of the Arroyo Seco. These 'improvements,' as they were called, allowed greater access to Los Angeles, which bolstered Pasadena's struggling economy.

"All of the improvements were constructed by local men under Scoville's employment program, which paid workers $1 a day – generous wages for the time, and a welcome paycheck for those men struggling to support their families during the economic depression. The plans for 'Scoville Park' serve as an example of one of the area's earliest 'public works' projects, benefitting not only individuals but the larger community as well.

"Sadly, James Scoville passed away suddenly in 1893, before the final details of construction on Scoville Park were completed. However, he lived long enough to see that his dream of a private park with public benefits would be realized. While his original park acreage has long since been subdivided, some tangible remnants of the park remain today, including the stone walls that grace the property at Arroyo del Rey – once the site of the park's stone barn."

Thus Heather had given us another example that the final structure was not, is not, the only important aspect of building a home. The process itself is the destination. And though it may seem a contradiction in terms, the process is the stability.

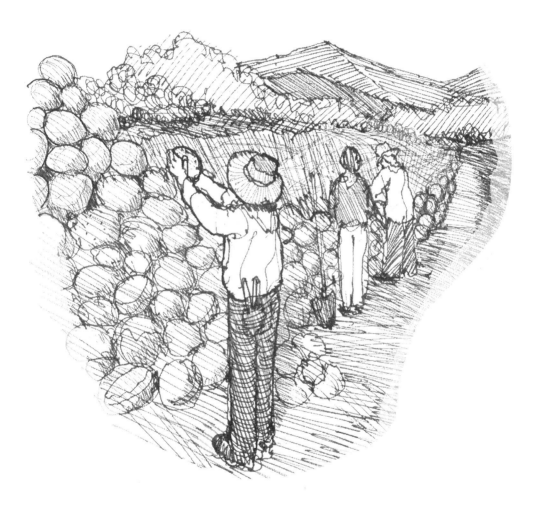

Nineteenth century workers building the stone walls that continue to grace Arroyo del Rey

YOU AND STABILITY...

Your stability depends on understanding that the important
thing in your life is the journey, not the destination.

For whatever you make to be of value,
it must not be divorced from the world of ideas.

The professional, social and personal aspects of your life
should all express who you really are.

The perfect home starts with being at home with yourself.

Acquire no more than you can care for with ease and harmony.

TALE II In the Garden
GROWTH

Hold me tight, oh garden scene,
Don't let me miss a single thing –
No leaf, no flower – earth's power pristine.
Oh nurturing land, teach me to dream!

The breeze enlivens all the paths
By gracefully swaying the fountain grass
And tripling acacias' rhythmic stance.
Oh gentle wind, teach me to dance!

The mockingbirds do beckon me
With joyous notes while soaring free
In melodious flight throughout the spring.
Oh wondrous choir, teach me to sing!

Infuse my spirit. Erase my cares.
My thoughts too filled with doubt and fears.
And bring them back to me refreshed.
Better this day than years of rest!

Hold me tight, oh garden scene,
Oh nurturing land, teach me to dream!

Gardens serve as metaphors for our deepest needs and highest yearnings. Visitors to Arroyo del Rey often ascribe non-visual meanings to the juxtaposition of our garden's quiet simplicity of the primarily green vegetation with the pre-existing bridges cutting across the northern and southern skies. Their interpretations are frequently quite similar to what Conrad and Don knew they were creating here – the contrast of the home and garden's serenity with the excitement of the bridges inspiring a sense of profound awe.

"There is something so amazingly brave in the idea of house and garden set in the shadow of modernity [the 134 freeway bridge] and yet wrapped in the arms of nature," wrote Mary Wildavsky after the Bay Area Horticultural Society's 2010 tour of Arroyo del Rey. "Forgive me for perhaps seeming somewhat hyperbolic – but that is how it struck me. There was truly a wonderful peace everywhere. Green gardens are relatively rare, but they are so restful."

LETTING NATURE SERVE AS METAPHOR FOR ALL OF LIFE

June Li, Curator of the Chinese Garden

The Huntington Library and Gardens

THE SALON ON THE SPIRITUALLY CREATIVE LIFE, MARCH 2007

"Liu Fang Yuan, the 'Garden of Flowing Fragrance,' is a special retreat within the magnificent grounds of the Huntington Library, Art Collections and Botanical Gardens in San Marino, California. Tracery windows set in an undulating wall reveal glimpses of a separate world of Chinese pavilions, stone bridges, and open terraces. Fantastic limestone rocks from Tai Hu in China are set against a one-acre lake. Hundred-year-old native California oaks, pines, and bamboo surround the enclosure. Three islands - the 'Isle of Alighting Geese,' 'Mandarin Ducks Island,' and 'Isle for Welcoming Cranes' – honor the garden's winged visitors - majestic egrets and herons, as well as cormorants, geese and ducks. A large open courtyard named the 'Terrace that Invites the Mountains' encompasses the distant San Gabriel Mountains as part of the garden's scenic offerings.

Limestone rock from Tai Hu

"Poetic names and verses in the form of Chinese calligraphy evoke the legendary scholars and poets of the past, inspiring the present with history and virtue. They complete the artistic expressions in the garden just as inscriptions do in a Chinese landscape painting, or *shan-shui-hua*. *Shan-shui*, or 'mountains – water,' describes the duality of the universe that balances the everlasting – rock – with the ever-changing – water. In the garden, the *taihu* rocks and the water of the lake represent these opposing yet complementary forces, signifying a microcosm uniting art, literature, and nature.

"In the depths of a canyon lush with camellias, magnolias and plums, a solitary thatched roof pavilion stands detached from the garden structures. Named the 'Pavilion for Washing Away Thoughts,' it exemplifies the hermit's simplicity and meditative spirit. All around, the refreshing scents of plants native to China perfume the air, evoking the original inspiration for the garden's creation and its name.

"The King residence, Arroyo del Rey, is also very much a world in itself. Like the Pavilion for Washing Away Thoughts, it is detached and tucked away in the Arroyo Seco, bordered by the cleansing waters of a nearby creek. Boulders and rocks complete its microcosm of flora and lushness all around. Winding trails of railroad ties are reminders of our participation in the wonders of this miniature universe."

Pavilion for Washing Away Thoughts
Huntington Library and Gardens

Just as nature is a superb teacher, so too are the outstanding individuals who cross our paths and share whatever insights they have gleaned from life.

LOVE: THE SUM OF MY LIFE

Author/Futurist Ray Bradbury

THE SALON ON THE SPIRITUALLY CREATIVE LIFE, JANUARY 2007

"I love Richard and Carol's house. I love this garden. I love speaking to The Salon on the Spiritually Creative Life. And that is why I am here – and that is what I give to you. Do something you love every day. Even when you think you can't.

Ray Bradbury

"Nine years ago, I had a stroke, and I tried as hard as I could. I found there is only one way to handle a stroke. And I would tell anyone who has a stroke to do something you love.

"I was in the hospital in Palm Springs for one day, and they brought me into St. John's Hospital in Santa Monica. I called my daughter Alexandra immediately and said, 'bring over the half-finished novel I'm working on. I need to do one hundred pages more. Right now. So sit there and take the dictation.'

"So every day, for eighty days, I dictated four pages of my mystery novel, *Let's All Kill Constance*. And I finished it in the hospital with a stroke. I was getting well. I was taking medicine. I was going to the gymnasium to work out. But what really led me through all this was my love for the work I was doing.

"I said, 'To hell with the stroke.' Instead I brought all my attention to the novel I was writing. God helped me finish the novel and deliver it and publish it.

"And that's what I give to you. If something like a stroke has knocked you down, do something that you love every day. Something that you were working on a few days ago and must continue now. Something that you love. Because that love will sustain you and heal you. I guarantee this."

To Ray Bradbury, author/poet/playwright who has set our fantasies soaring on the wings of such books as *The Martian Chronicles* and *Fahrenheit 451*, Love is life's main ingredient, the power behind everything good we can experience. Having spoken before The Salon every year since its beginning, the subject always revolved around the Love he felt in his heart. Ray told how this Love propelled him and his life itself until his dreams came true – whether they were of the people he admired and wished to meet or of types of writing he had yet to publish on subjects such as dinosaurs, Martians and world fairs.

At one such salon, just before Ray's eighty-seventh birthday, he was seated in his usual armchair in our living room and he seemed that day as "exuberant as a flight of larks." These were the words used to describe

Ray Bradbury's writing style by the American art critic Bernard Berenson [1865-1959], regarded during his life as the world's foremost expert on the Italian Renaissance. Those words seemed apt not only for Ray Bradbury's use of words but also for the total presence of Ray Bradbury the man, particularly on this day.

"Profit is in the heart," Ray said, warning us to follow nothing and no one who would lead us to look elsewhere. "They would keep you from being you, interfering with your Loves.

"Turn back to your own list of Loves, and listen not to strangers but to what is *here*," he said, his hand over his heart.

It was a fitting message at that Salon in particular, as the highly recognized sculptor Christopher Slatoff had just unveiled in the midst of our living room his first completed sculpture of Ray. Only it was not just Ray.

"I am not me," Ray had said when I had first suggested to Ray that Chris create a sculpture of him, "I am my father."

During the following months, Ray further explained to Chris what he meant by this – that his being infused with his father's constant Love and understanding when Ray was a young boy is what enabled him to realize his true identity. In this, Ray found complete accord in Chris, who himself felt deeply indebted to his own father for providing him wings for his own accomplishments.

Ray was Ray's father because his father understood that his son loved certain things even when he, the father, did not particularly love the same things with the same enthusiasm. Ray was his father because it was his father who carried the child Ray forward - to the library, to the circus, to all the places his father knew his son longed to be. Weekend after weekend when he was growing up, Ray remembered his father tirelessly taking him forth until the child Ray would be satiated with so many wondrous delights that he would fall asleep in his father's arms.

Ray Bradbury leads Salon overseen by Christopher Statoff's sculpture

Finally at The Salon, when Chris threw off the canvas and revealed the figure which he had been developing during this period in his studio, we could see that Chris had translated Ray's memories into clay. The father carrying his son Ray forth to his fields of dreams had become Chris's marble-dusted creation.

On the sculpted father's back was an intertwining galaxy of earthen characters cascading down neck to legs, embodying Ray Bradbury's future stories, plays and novels - a summation of *The Illustrated Man* and of all Ray's carnival-fantasy-Martian-filled odes to the garden that is our Life.

AT HOME WITH
ALEX AND JAYLENE MOSELEY

Alex Moseley, Artist/Designer

Founding Member Flintridge Center

THE SALON ON THE SPIRITUALLY CREATIVE LIFE, AUGUST 2000

It was a quintessential example of the understated, unassuming, Don Hensman. I asked him if he could speak at The Salon and have us gather this time, not at Arroyo del Rey but in the home he had just completed for his clients and good friends, Alex and Jaylene Moseley. Don's lifelong architect partner Conrad Buff, with whom he had built the Moseleys' previous home, had passed away, and this home, built near ours but set high above the Arroyo instead of within it, Don had designed solo.

"Sure," said Don. Then, on the morning of The Salon, Don, always one to shine the spotlight on others rather than himself, especially when they were people he admired and trusted, turned much of the entire program over to Alex.

But, then, in many ways, Alex Moseley was Don Hensman's twin, and he directed the light right back on Don – a fitting tribute for the creative sensitivity and architectural genius that is the Buff & Hensman legacy.

Conrad Buff III   Don Hensman

Looking directly at Don, Alex said: "As we slip through life, we react to mundane, exciting and sometimes anxious encounters. Our responses come and go like clouds, but over time they delineate the form of our expectations and life's possibilities. Yet every now and then there's the rare and unexpected and transformative encounter. They are surprising or unwitting connections that spark without notice and affect without warning. These encounters are assimilated and change your perceptions, engage your consciousness and illuminate new paths of possibility.

Alex and Jaylene Moseley gaze up at their home completed by Don Hensman in 1999

"Such an encounter is part of the gift when working with architects Conrad Buff III and Donald Hensman. These two great individuals created the Kings' residence, and now Don has created this home for Jaylene and myself – both perfect gathering places for The Salon's concentration on positive uplifted thought – perfect because of the ideals that Conrad and Don's architecture expressed and that they as human beings expressed.

"Their classic but unpretentious designs belie a profound determination for the correctness and appropriateness of a solution. Inherently, they knew the energy applied up front, to a sensitively thought out and correctly detailed decision, would reflect back as calmness and serenity to the living spaces and the lives of the residents. From the way the house is set on the property to the great feel of the building and space proportions, there is a sense of common trust and understanding transmitted between the designers, the residents and the surroundings.

"There is a level of detail in life that nervously cries for attention – busyness always begging, and never satisfied with the attention. There is another level of detail, no less involved, that projects an air of calm in its correctness. Creating the latter was the consummate skill of architects Conrad Buff III and Donald Hensman.

"The exquisite and warm qualities of what they created exude an encouragement for personal expression, fellowship and the capturing of new opportunity. Their works of architecture, as they themselves have done personally, bring out the best in the lives of the families that dwell inside their creations and creativity. Their architecture cultivates growth."

YOU AND GROWTH...

Celebrate personal expression,
fellowship and new opportunity.

Tend whatever you have with
care, patience and Love.

No matter how small, take nothing
in your world for granted.

Recognize the difference between that which is
everlasting and that which is ever-changing.

Listen to what you love and let it
sustain and heal you.

Native American Spiritual Leader Hua Anwa leads the Salon.

TALE III At the Water's Edge
POSSIBILITY

Life gushes forth. Life full of Love.
Yet frictionless past it can seem to glide,
Leaving the timid midst stillborn pool
While enraptured others sail happily by.

Instead, command your vessel!
Navigate each day with conscious thought!
Mentally anoint yourself and others
With joy, strength and, above all, Love!

Believe. Wake up in the morning and believe that you have something special to do, something special to say, something special to create. You have something to express that no one else on earth can express in just the same way. This is your purpose. Your innate being gives you the courage, the energy and the constancy to achieve what you are meant to do during this period of your being, during this period of your life on earth.

As long as we are on this planet in these bodies, we must understand that we are given this earthly experience to learn something, and not just to *try* but to *do*. That is the only value of being here on this plane of existence. While we are here, in this form, we must *take action*. We must serve the individual intention that resides in each of us. We all are given a path and we must take that journey.

LIVING A LIFE OF POSSIBILITY

Hua Anwa

Native American Spiritual Leader

THE SALON ON THE SPIRITUALLY CREATIVE LIFE, JULY 2009

"Living a creative spiritual life is living a life of possibility. When we gather as a community for spiritual enrichment, as we are gathered in Richard and Carol King's inspirational home and garden today, we are elevating the whole and keeping ourselves healthy.

"When we lived in circles we had common ground, a Sacred place where we could go and commune with the Great Spirit or the creative force. A Sacred place is a space of welcome for all to gather for renewal, inspiration, spiritual nourishment, and to drink from the well of oneness, for when we practice an environment of equality, it fosters tolerance, unconditional love and harmony. There is no one left out. When neighboring communities came for a visit, we knew we would be judged by the way we carry our community, how we care for our Sacred grounds and the ones who have the least.

"A meaningful life in harmony with fellow humans and nature is our goal, knowing that we gain a freedom when we embrace our spiritual creativity, for there is hope of evolution of our spirit selves as a collective.

"There is a tradition called 'The Twisted Hairs.' The hair symbolizes knowledge, and the Twisted Hairs are those who weave knowledge from all sources into the braid of wisdom. The Twisted Hairs society walked outside of their tribal boundaries, their traditional teachings. They chose to seek knowledge from many sources beyond the confines of their community in order to develop their mastery of the physical world, to awaken their spirit, to develop as complete human beings, to become enlightened, and to have spiritual power.

"AHO!"
(Native American for Amen)

"Today, as in the past, we come together to openly exchange the various sources of knowledge, thus transcending only one point of view and elevating ourselves collectively with truths, wisdom and knowledge. The ultimate expressions of our humanness are our choices to gather together, to share with one another, to teach one another, care for one another, love one another, and be open with one another in heart-to-heart communication. These teachings of the Twisted Hairs show us how to come together in a circle of brothers and sisters.

"We have a saying, 'to all my relations.' We are all related to one another. We have one common mother, The Earth Mother. Therefore, we are always HOME. As we stand with open HEART and open MINDS, we will always be HOME. AHO!"

When we underestimate our own power, we ourselves become the only real obstacle to our rightful destiny. We must remember that the innate longings of our inner beings are there for a purpose beyond our personal lives. So when we assert what we truly believe, there is no doubt that we will better our lives and the lives of others.

We are and always have been like diamonds, formed in the womb of Love long before human birth, with all the beauty and perfection of a diamond and with an indestructible strength. The basis of who we are will never change – it always was and always will be the same. As long as we forget this, our real heritage, we forsake the chance to acknowledge and express the continuity of our birthright to its fullest degree.

I like to encourage others to speak up for themselves, to put themselves in the running – for I see how incredibly valuable they are, how much they have to give, and how awesomely great their talent. "Love yourself! Don't be afraid! Do it!" I urge them. Yet at the same time I know that often it has been difficult to do this for myself. I have cowered under the illusion that I might not be good enough. Good enough for what? As soon as I could tell myself, "Just be good enough to love what I do and good enough to try," then I can feel the wind under my wings.

MAY YOU ALWAYS BE FREE

Nan Rae, Artist

THE SALON ON THE SPIRITUALLY CREATIVE LIFE, NOVEMBER 2006

Are there strings that bind you? What are they? What is their nature? How did they get there? When did you first feel they were holding you back? Are they real? Are they so strong that they cannot be broken?

These are some of the questions artist Nan Rae brought to those of us gathered one Sunday for The Salon. Her husband, Charles Parker, had just read aloud an intriguing little book, *Suma the Elephant* by Gary Shoup, which Nan had illustrated with her elegant and sensitive Chinese brush paintings.

It is a parable for children of all ages. And we all were like enraptured children as we sat at Charles' feet, listening as his strong, low, resonant voice carried us deep into the world of the baby elephant Suma who was captured by monkeys to make her a pet. The monkeys tie her to a tree, and since she is so little, they use nothing but strings. The tree provides shade, and leaves from nearby bushes and the grass growing under the tree give her sustenance, and puddles from the area's frequent rains allow her enough to drink. However, as Suma starts to grow into her massive, intelligent adulthood and tries to walk further

Although now big and mighty, Suma believes the strings still keep her from being free.

than the strings would permit, the monkeys drop coconuts on her head to stop her. As each coconut finds its mark, Suma retreats even further from expressing her own native power and majesty. Even after the monkeys move on and leave her alone to fend for herself, and even when other elephants pass by inviting her to join them on their journeys, the memory of the monkeys' mocking laughter and the pain of those dropping coconuts keep her from even trying to tug at the strings. Mighty as Suma is in size and ability, she still thinks of herself as only a pet and is unable to break free. At the story's end, she is still utterly trapped through her emotional imprisonment, able only to wistfully dream of what she already possesses.

"Will Suma break the strings that bind her?" Nan Rae asked, looking at each and every one of her spellbound fans. "What are the emotional strings of intimidation with which we ourselves are entangled? And can we break them?"

The answer to Nan Rae is that we definitely can: "How well this illustrates that the strings that bind us are only that – strings! Nothing stronger than that is holding us back! If we only break these strings and open ourselves to the universe, we will be gifted with all manner of creativity and wonder.

"Finally," Nan concluded, "what if I told you it is impossible for you to fail?"

Without success when they invite the emotionally imprisoned Suma to join them, the other elephants prepare to journey on without her.

And then, asking her audience to see the situation from yet another perspective, Nan suggested that, at times, we ourselves might be the monkeys – the ones who put the strings on others. Even as we go about trying to live as well as we can and going along with the flow of what seem to be good intentions, we inflict harm to others when no harm was meant. This can be the most disheartening of moments, to realize that, no matter if unintentionally, we have wronged another. Yet the very realization of this means ... what? It means that we can understand, and, yes, even *love* the monkeys!

Suma's story reminds us all to break those imaginary strings that would prevent us from living up to our potential right now. We do not have to believe in all those things that others say will hold us down. The entire potential of the universe is our bottomless well from which to draw. All strength, all insight, all understanding is ours right now. This well of universal potential will never run dry and will always continue to enlighten our understanding and empower our way.

We do not have to wait until we have more money. We do not have to wait until we have a different job. We do not have to wait for the right personal circumstance. We can express our true self right now, for our true identity is all that exists and all that can have any real effect.

OPENING OUR HEARTS TO THE TREASURE OF INTERCONNECTIVITY

Tobey Crockett, PhD

Artist, Theorist, Virtual Visionary

THE SALON ON THE SPIRITUALLY CREATIVE LIFE, JULY 2009

"I always consider myself to be quite fortunate to have been the first speaker in the series of enriching talks at Carol and Richard King's wonderful Salon. Later, I attended quite often and was honored to be featured as the guest speaker several times, during which I would offer variations on my special theme of interconnectivity.

"Whether seen from a philosophical, humanist or scientific perspective, it becomes increasingly clear that the world in which we live is part of a larger, entangled and intertwined reality, a multivalent fabric in which every tiny smidgen of consciousness plays a vital role in reflecting and manifesting the whole. One way to think of this is as a holographic paradigm; there is no independent arising, and yet each one of us has a unique voice, perspective and story to share; we are indivisible from one another, while retaining our own identity. It is a kind of sweet paradox.

"Tracing this line of thinking further into the 21st century, I like to suggest that the primary metaphor offered to us by the interactive revolution is that we occupy a newly digitalized and pixilated paradigm. In that paradigm every bit of information is now even further empowered to speak for itself, and is, in a specific sense, even required to participate.

"An excellent example of this shift can be found in the spectacular scenes that are created in special effects films. In a fully digitized volume, there are no blank spaces, there is no emptiness, indeed, even the spots that appear as empty are in fact only masquerading as void.

"Even though the magic of movies is an apparently frivolous place for deep philosophy to begin, we can observe in this cinema of the spectacular that every iota is activated, authorized and enabled for transmission. Every point has agency. In a new take on Nietzsche's famous remark, the abyss indeed looks back. The implications for our human society are profound.

"Focusing on creating healthy, diverse and vibrant communities, both online and in the real world, we can rise to the occasion to build a better world. Our human project, to compose an ever more complete and wisdom-infused picture of our actual reality and lived lives, requires a clarity and elegant turn of thought that is deceptively simple in its precision.

"Such deep thinking is best fostered in the spirit of community and creativity, in the open heart of our compassionate ability to listen to others, and by simply holding space for the perfect beings that are our companions on this human journey. We do this by allowing ourselves and those around us to share their authentic story, by participating in the hard work of making positive change, and by staking a claim to caring about the things that count: connection to friends and family, participation on a local level, and being of service to the needs and dreams of others.

Richard and Gypsy retreat to the Gazebo.

"To be rich in relationship is the greatest treasure of all and we are fortunate that we *already exist* in a wonderful web of interconnection. We need only open our eyes and hearts to see that it is so."

YOU AND POSSIBILITY...

Know that you gain freedom when you embrace your spirituality.

Love yourself! Don't be afraid! Do it!

Remember that the "strings" that bind you are only that - strings!

You already exist in a wonderful web of interconnectivity.

Recognize the difference between "try" and "do."

Remember that the innate longings of your inner being are there for a purpose beyond your personal life.

TALE IV Maintaining the Grounds
HUMOR

Early here one morning,
On the eastern side of town,
A little girl came running up
The hill and then came down.

It was a game of tag she played there,
And she was winning, I could tell.
The sun had chased her to this valley
And still was chasing when she fell.

From my hiding place I watched them,
Never such I've ever seen.
For the sun, who soon caught up,
Began to lend the brightest sheen.

Then he tapped her, very softly,
On her shoulder near the ground,
And, when she rose, he beamed on past her –
Their game of chase re-found.

Our Betta fish at play with his carved wooden companion

We have so much to learn from children. They innately pay homage to play, humor, lightness. They understand intuitively that every moment can be filled with joy. Animals embody this childlike spirit, too - our dog Gypsy's constant delight in simply living, the numerous raccoons, rabbits, and squirrels that try non-stop to entice Gypsy with their games of hide and seek. Even our Betta fish, whom we call The Emperor, responds to the life around his aquarium, our Alvar Aalto-designed vase, with unmistakable enthusiasm.

How easy it would be to bid farewell to tension, stress and anxiety, if we only would infuse our days with joy rather than letting our days infuse us with concern. All we have to do to empower the space which surrounds us is to respond to Love's unending sunshine - as other more innocent members of the animal kingdom do, as children do, as we when we were children did!

METAPHORS: BREAKFAST OF CHAMPIONS

Author/Futurist Ray Bradbury

THE SALON ON THE SPIRITUALLY CREATIVE LIFE, SEPTEMBER 2004

"If you're not playing with life all the time, it's not worth living," said author/futurist Ray Bradbury, a man who maintained throughout his life a child-like freshness in all that he did. Ray's excitement grew with each sentence – each idea compelling the next and surpassing the one before in his joy-filled fantasies.

"That's what's so incredible about science fiction and one of its main lessons," said the beloved creator of hundreds of tales that are cautionary as well as fanciful. "As in science fiction, whatever you tackle in life should be playful! Play with philosophy, architecture, ecology, political science, urban planning, transportation, literature, poetry, theology ... everything. Even if you're self-educated, as I am, by the time you're 35, you will have a total education and you will have fun getting it! And you will help others by your positive example!

"It doesn't matter what your field is! The point is to unleash the joy!"

Comedian Bob Hope once told me during an interview for a story I was writing for Father's Day that, in his opinion, one of the most important aspects of being a good father – "or a good friend to anyone" – is taking time to talk. "Just talking can play a major part in letting these other important people in your life know they are loved and appreciated."

"The most important thing to do with your children is to rap with them," he said. "That's what my dad used to do with me. He used to sit me down – when he could catch me! – and try to find out what I was thinking. That's what I always tried to get my kids to do – to talk it over."

"Did it ever backfire?" I asked.

"Not really – but it surprised me once," Hope replied. "When my son Kelly was young, we had a little trouble because he was the youngest and most spoiled, and was always making faces at the table.

"One time I told him, 'Look! Stop that! Stop making faces at the table or you and I are going to go outside!'

"Well, about ten minutes later he made another face. So, I picked the little tyke up with one hand and started walking down the hall to go outside. But he stopped me in my tracks when he said, 'Hey, Dad, I think we oughta talk this over!'

"There was never any trouble after that," said Bob Hope. "He always wanted to talk it over."

A sense of humor, so apparent in Bob Hope's story, is also vital in maintaining a loving relationship. For that same Father's Day story, former child film star Shirley Temple Black recalled how her father's excellent sense of humor enhanced her entire life.

"His being able to keep things light not only brought out my own personality so much that I could handle comic roles at the age of three," she told me. "His sense of fun also enabled my family to get through the most trying of circumstances.

Shirley Temple at 8

"For example," she said, "one morning on our first Hawaiian trip, which was in 1935, my parents and I were having breakfast on the Royal Hawaiian's lanai. My father, wearing the first dressy white jacket he had ever owned, had just received his fried eggs.

"From out of nowhere, a fan rushed up to me and, in the process, since fans never notice anyone else is present, brushed Dad's eggs all over his jacket.

"But instead of getting angry, Dad just laughed and said, 'Guess we'll have to send it to the cleaners,' and smiled brightly at the dismayed young woman who had created the mess. 'Not our sense of humor. The jacket!'"

'ANGELS CAN FLY 'CAUSE THEY TAKE THEMSELVES LIGHTLY': HUMOR AND SPIRITUALITY

BJ Gallager, Author / Inspirational Speaker
THE SALON ON THE SPIRITUALLY CREATIVE LIFE, OCTOBER 2009

"G.K. Chesterton wrote, 'Angels can fly 'cause they take themselves lightly.' But we humans seem to get our knickers in a twist about stuff that doesn't matter one whit in the cosmic scheme of things. We often make much ado about nothing ... turning molehills into mountains... and the inconsequential into the monumental. (Sigh.) What a silly species we are!

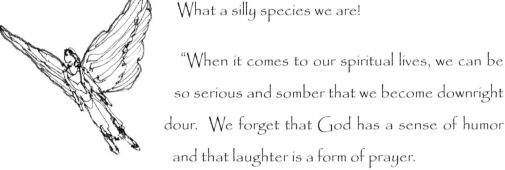

"When it comes to our spiritual lives, we can be so serious and somber that we become downright dour. We forget that God has a sense of humor and that laughter is a form of prayer.

"What can we do to become more like angels and take ourselves lightly? Here are just a few of the many ideas to explore at The Salon today:

"Give others the benefit of the doubt. We humans have a double standard. We judge ourselves by our intentions, but we judge others by their actions. If I inadvertently say or do something that hurts your feelings, I explain that 'my intentions were good – I didn't mean to be hurtful.' But if you say or do something that hurts me, I assume the worst and give no thought to your intentions – I judge you solely on your behavior. We would all do well to give others the same benefit of the doubt that we give ourselves and give them credit for good intentions.

"<u>Don't sweat the small stuff.</u> I know it sounds like a cliché, but it's so true. Most of life is small stuff – yet we lose our cool over the most trivial things: someone cutting us off in traffic, someone with too many items in their grocery cart while standing in the express checkout line, a customer service person who doesn't use the tone of voice we think is appropriate, a friend who doesn't return our phone call promptly, someone who's chronically late for meetings and appointments. Ohmygosh, are we so perfect that we should judge others so harshly ... and for such trivial things?!

"<u>Celebrate what's right with the world.</u> The mind is a mismatch detector; it always notices what's wrong before it sees what's right. This makes us inclined to focus on flaws, foibles, mistakes, and things gone awry ... while overlooking the myriad good things around us. We walk into a gallery with ten paintings on the wall and our eyes go immediately to the one that's hanging slightly askew. Our child brings home a report card with one bad grade and all the rest good grades ... and what do we focus on? The bad grade. Everybody's a critic. We would do ourselves and our loved ones a HUGE favor by retraining our minds to look for what's right with the world ... and celebrate it!

"We could all experience a little more of our Heavenly Garden on Earth if we'd take a cue from the cherubim and seraphim ... and take ourselves lightly. Ask yourself on a regular basis: Have I laughed at myself today?"

If you are blessed with a sense of humor, one of the best ways to keep it in top form is not to be tired, not to be late, and to be prepared – plus a few extra minutes to draw a deep breath. In other words, keeping your joyous, loving spirit in shape requires keeping your personal garden in shape.

Phyllis Diller

I will never forget Phyllis Diller's answer when once I asked that inveterate comedienne, renowned for never letting her audiences down, how she always manages to put her best foot forward when in the spotlight.

"You should know what you're doing and check all the last minute details so there are no last minute crises or, as we call them in my business, no 'surprises,'" she told me. "You should provide yourself with everything you need and not depend on other people. All important is to give yourself plenty of time ahead for interruptions, phone calls, broken zippers, flat tires – those things people think are such great excuses for being late, for not being ready. Give yourself enough time so you never have to apologize – so boring! – and so you never wind up on the wrong end of the stick.

"The ideal preparation," she added, "includes leaving yourself enough time so that, after you've gotten everything else ready for the big event, you'll have time to sit quietly and compose your own mind and body."

As I recall were Phyllis Diller's parting words that day, "Life is a do-it-yourself kit and you're the head kitten. So get in there and scratch!"

One day when the ever headstrong Gypsy was taking me for a walk, I noticed our neighbor Laura out by her gate, scraping off the paint on her mailbox so she could replace it with a fresh coat.

"You already have the best mail box on the street," I commented.

"I know, but I do enjoy the caretaker part of my being," she joyfully replied.

"You really are an inspiration," I told her, looking beyond her to her immaculately kept house, always in perfect order despite her sizable family and full-time job. "How do you do all you do?"

"Oh, it's nothing at all," she replied modestly. Somehow there's a spiritual quality in taking care of one's possessions, at least when I take care of them with a peaceful feeling and allow my thinking to be directed toward the ones I love. When I do, each task becomes less like a chore and more like a love song.

"Besides, leave your home a mess, and what right have you to expect more from the world beyond?

"Then, too, keeping your possessions in order yourself is beneficial to you psychologically and spiritually. You make yourself feel capable of establishing harmony, of taking care of what you have, of accomplishing something positive. It's self-reliance, and self-reliance is really a matter of self-respect!

"People can discuss beauty all their lives. But if they don't express joy in making even the simplest things more orderly and clean, if they don't have fun in making things beautiful, what do they really know?"

To buoy my journey into the garden and beyond, for there is nothing like walking side by side, Richard and Gypsy join me. From time to

Richard, Carol, and Gypsy share a delicious moment...

time gently brushing against each other, always aware of each other's breathing, ours is a delicious partnership. As much as it was Conrad and Don's sensitive design, it also is our passion and compassion for each other that have empowered this place, as through Love's prism all that graces our path reveals its glowing aura. And then I look at Richard and he is beaming.

We watch the ducks paddle down the creek, the scrub jays dive for nuts in our outstretched hands, and the tree squirrels leap from limb to limb as if only to mischievously tempt Gypsy with their game of chase. We are enveloped by the sand toads' full-throated vibrato and even catch sight of a raccoon ready to challenge *us* for trespassing in *his* sanctuary. And then Richard winks at me and I burst into non-stop giggles.

With Love as our guide, we can experience, even now on this planet, that which is ours for eternity – the joy of living and the lightness of being. Yes, lightness! And it will include many smiles! Lots of laughter!

YOU AND HUMOR...

Infuse your day with joy! Even homemaking and caretaking can be fun - it's just a matter of perspective.

Poke fun at upsets.

Hold onto your loves and let them play throughout your life!

Forget what's wrong! Celebrate what's right!

Don't let momentary anger stand in your way. Talk things over!

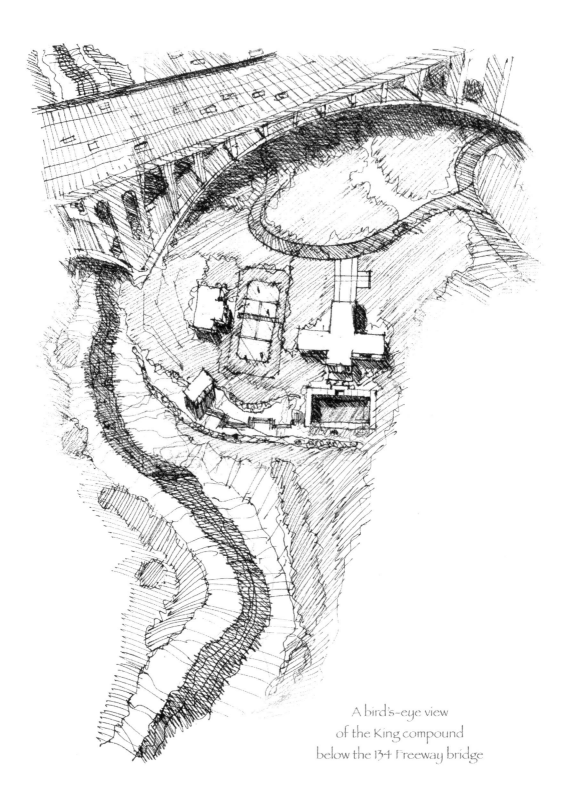

A bird's-eye view of the King compound below the 134 Freeway bridge

TALE V Building Bridges
UNDERSTANDING

> Climb up! Climb up to soaring heights!
> And never look back, but onward go
> Until your goal you finally attain.
> Then turn 'round. Help others gain!

"Building Bridges" could not have been a more appropriate title for my husband Richard's Salon Presentation. The Emperor of Japan had just honored him with the Order of the Rising Sun with Golden Rays and Rosette for his more than five decades of building business, educational and cultural bridges between Japan and the United States. And indeed, it is to this type of bridge building between peoples and nations that Richard has devoted his entire professional career.

BUILDING BRIDGES: UNDERSTANDING SPIRITUALITY AT WORK

Richard King, HonDB

Chairman/Founder of King International Group
Co-Founder, Business Renaissance Institute and GoGreen Solutions

THE SALON ON THE SPIRITUALLY CREATIVE LIFE, OCTOBER 2000

Richard's medal from the Emperor of Japan

"I'd like to discuss the subject of spirituality in a broader sense. Spirituality is often confused with religion. They are two different things. Spirituality is more inward and what we're about internally. Religion is more external.

"I think there are some key elements in this subject of spirituality. I co-authored a few books on 'Spirituality in the Workplace.' But spirituality is really more than the workplace – it is who we are, what we are, the meaning in our lives, the interconnectedness we feel with the universe. These are all components of spirituality as we know it. And spirituality is also related very much to universality. Everything is connected and interconnectedness is a very key term.

"I recall recently there was a research program done at Stanford Business School in which they were identifying different categories of behavior: the traditionalists, the modernists, and a new one called 'the cultural creatives.' And the cultural creatives are people who are interested in sustainable development, care of the elderly, things that are components of spirituality. And they found sixty-five million people in the United States who feel this way.

"But each of them feels that he or she is unique, the only one thinking that way. So I thought that was a very interesting study. It points out the need for interconnectedness. We have to know what each other is thinking, and connect ourselves to others, not only individually but corporately, culturally, and internationally. We have to build bridges. What we are all here for is to build bridges in our own way, build bridges to others, through understanding and through love – and through giving people meaning in their lives.

Following his Salon presentation, Richard and a few associates continue discussing how building bridges between all aspects of our lives can pave the way for a truly integrated experience.

"In my study in the book *Spirituality in the Workplace* [co-authored with Joan Marques, PhD and Satinder Dhiman, PhD], most people are looking for meaning in their work and meaning in their lives. It is very interesting to me that many studies on people's attitude in the workplace show that fifty percent of the respondents are unhappy in their work. And you ask why are they unhappy? Well, they're not appreciated, they're not recognized, they find no meaning in their work and their work is so much a part of their lives that they have no meaning in their existence.

"So what I talk about, feel strongly about, is that we must do things that do provide meaning in people's lives, meaning in their work. So they can be more productive, they can enhance the quality of life on the planet. So they can take themselves to a higher dimension of productivity, of vision, of creativity. And when you think about it, that's just good business. People who are happy and content and harmonious are going to be more productive and creative, and that is going to impact productivity and return on investment. These things are very important.

"I think also this factor of core values and finding out who we are is important. People don't know who they are – and before you can do anything with your life, you have to know who you are, what you want, what your priorities are. And it is important to establish that and then look at life as a journey. Because life really is a journey. Destinations aren't really that important. Enjoy the journey. Every day of it. And you enjoy that more if it's in a loving, harmonious, creative environment. So I think that is very important – giving more meaning to life, more productivity, more vision.

"I think also the factor of values is very important. Values. You know each of us is only one person. We're not a good guy at the office and a bad guy at home, or vice versa. Each of us is one person. I always like to use the term 'oneness.' There is a oneness about being, and you have to carry those core values through every aspect of your life no matter what you are doing. I know many executives who tend to separate their business life from their personal life. But I always tell people you can't check your values at the door. You have to take your values with you, into the workplace.

"And if you have good core values and take them with you, you would be surprised at what impact that might have on the environment. You are not, cannot be, a different person in your home environment, your work environment and your extended environment. You have to reflect on that – who are you? What are your priorities? What are you doing with your life? And have a passion for what you're doing.

"I keep getting back to the journey. It's the journey, not the destination, that's important.

"And finally I think we have to remember that we are all connected spirits. We are spirits. Someone once said we are not humans on a spiritual journey, we are spirits on a human journey. And this is exactly true. This stop on this planet is just one part of the continuous aspect in the universality of our life. So we have to be the best and most developed spirits that we can be and make a difference and have an impact on our environment.

"So perhaps we are all on the planet to enhance the quality of life on Earth and make it better when we leave than when we came in. And to do that, understanding our spirituality is key."

Following Richard's Salon presentation, a middle-aged Cuban named Luis, whose loose shirt sleeves revealed that he had no arms, asked if he could speak with me. Nothing could have pleased me more – for I was well aware that Luis, despite overwhelming obstacles, had just received his university degree in Los Angeles. I was equally eager to speak with him.

"I am so inspired by Dr. King's urging all of us to serve others by building bridges of understanding," he said. "Yet, I still feel so emotional about my own past hardships. I am thankful for what I have today, but sometimes the past just wells up unannounced. It feels negative, as if I am feeling sorry for myself, and I certainly do not want to be. So, I am wondering if we could spend some time over at your studio, with you as catcher of my thoughts."

Of course, I immediately said "yes" and the two of us, with Gypsy at our side as always, walked to the Pavilion where I do my writing. Its sequestered location beyond the tennis court is on a plateau that is at once nestled under the bridges yet high enough to look down on our property's eastern stone walls with the creek farther below. From each of its private gardens encircling its heather-and-mauve painted stucco walls, it offers an idyllic vantage point from which to view the world and consider our place within it. Today, even with two of the lingering salon guests having started to play a game of tennis, it was the ideal place for me to be "catcher" of Luis's reveries.

Luis, Carol, and Gypsy at the Pavilion

In receiving his degree, Luis, a recent immigrant to the United States, said it was not surprising to have heard murmurs in the crowd of "Isn't it amazing?" … "You're unbelievable" … and so on. These were the sort of comments to which he had become accustomed. Yet for years, Luis, deserving as he was of such accolades, could never feel he truly warranted such praise. He felt that it stemmed from people's sympathy for what they viewed as his pathetic physical situation.

The 47-year-old Luis was born with only partially formed arms – mere stumps at each shoulder. No reasons for this happenstance were ever determined. Worse, he was born so sickly that the doctors felt he should be allowed to die.

Only one man disagreed. His father.

From then on, Luis credits his entire life and the remarkable feats entailed in overcoming his disabilities to his father's faith, patience and understanding of Love.

His father had just graduated from medical school when his son was born in a little town in Cuba.

"He was a very religious man," said his son. "He felt my life had to be saved."

Although his son was on the critical list for six months, Luis's father was sure he could find a way to help him survive, even if he had to use new and untried medicines. In the end, he was successful. Only it wasn't those medicines that had helped. The cure lay in this wise father's heart and his huge doses of Love.

When Luis was 2-years-old and still could not walk, the doctors insisted he never would be able to walk normally. Again, Luis's father refused to listen.

"When I was 4-years-old, I thought I would attempt walking but fell each time I tried. Everyone - my mother, my older brother, friends - wanted to help me. But my father kept them all at a distance. 'Don't touch him. He has to learn by himself.'

"Soon," said Luis, "I was able to walk by myself.

Young Luis with his father

"When I was 7-years-old, I still couldn't read or write, and it had never occurred to anyone that I ever would. Anyone, that is, except my father.

"One day he called me into his office and asked, 'My son, you like to go to the movies, don't you?' knowing full well that I did, that I went every day of my otherwise narrow life, that I couldn't live without Ginger Rogers, Fred Astaire and Dracula.

"'Oh, yes, Papa!' I said, and he said, 'You are not to go one more time until you learn to write!'

"And everybody said, 'No! It's cruel! Don't make him suffer! He can't ever write! He can't ever do anything!'

"But my father said, 'My boy, I know you can do it. You *have* to find a way.'

"So the man next door said he could probably teach me how to write, and he began the very next day. In no time at all I had learned not only how to make these stumps guide a pencil on paper, but also how to read."

During those painful days of learning tasks so difficult for him, Luis said he did not realize how wise his father was.

"At that time I probably didn't even think I liked him," he recalls. "Because everyone else tried to baby me, my father was the one who had to force me to learn how to dress myself, to eat by myself, to do everything by myself.

The young Luis suffers ridicule.

" 'You have to learn,' my father said, 'because someday you will be alone.'

"Then, the most important lesson my father taught me came one day when I was 13-years-old. A girl had refused to dance with me at a party, because I was so ugly. I told my father I would never go to another party.

"But my father said, 'You must not back away. You have to love even when you are not loved. Because you are a cripple, you have to realize that many who are not crippled will not understand your situation. They may not like to be with you. They may make fun of you. The answer will always be that they do not understand you. But you do have the power to understand them and to see them surrounded with Love. If you do this, you will have gained rather than lost from being a cripple, for you will understand yourself.'"

Throughout Luis's teenage years, his father was always at his side – not protecting him, but showing him how to be independent of the hateful feelings that threatened to overtake him time and time again.

Finally, Luis was so grateful for what his father had given him that he himself volunteered to tutor other cripples at an institute for the physically challenged in Havana.

And later, when he was 19-years-old, Luis landed a paying job in Havana's City Hall. Three months later his father died, but his son, though born with no arms, was now able to give a helping hand to the many who came to him for assistance. As his father had said would be possible through understanding himself and not ceasing to share his understanding of Love with others, Luis had not lost but gained from being a cripple. And now he was turning around and helping others gain!

"So you see," Luis concluded, turning to me to see the effect of his life's story on my face, "I have been blessed. I have been allowed to succeed and even help others. But I sometimes still have doubts about the purpose of it all. Because the same kind of cruelty I faced keeps happening to those I try to help, and to others all over the world. Life can seem so futile."

I looked out at the garden and down at the gently flowing creek. Luis's doubts I too have known. Finally, I heard myself speaking. "Life

on earth really is but a crucible for getting rid of the dross and burnishing our gold. The challenges will always be there, for they are the avenue through which we can purify ourselves and assist others. If you can serve as a bridge to such understanding among those you are asked to teach and lead, you cannot ask for more. And that is what you are doing, Luis."

YOU AND UNDERSTANDING

You are meant to be a bridge between
your best self and others.

Your core values have to be carried
through every aspect of your life.

Return others' wrong attitudes
with understanding and Love.

Pursue the seamless life in which work,
play and loving relationships are one.

Whatever your circumstance, you can accept it,
learn from it, and help others.

Even the most severe disabilities
are no match for faith, patience and understanding.

Never say "can't"!

TALE VI *Our Real Estate*
KINDNESS

Everything drops away –

downward, outward –

And we take a trip on an elevated silence.

Separated by an invisible wall,

we look out.

Suddenly, everything is in harmony.

We are receptive to everything.

And we know

We are never

To be

The same

Again.

Carol and Gypsy on the sandbar

Gypsy leads the way, intent on the never-ending breezes wafting up from the creek with their myriad scents of the seen and unseen. I lie down on a sandbar just below the surface of the water, its caresses massaging my silt-covered form until I feel I am becoming one with its flow. At this moment of near immersion, I know that I and all of Life are inseparable. The depth of this metaphoric sensation is revealing to me how completely all of us are ensconced in a universe of gentle kindness.

MY MOMENT WITH MONTANA

Georgeanne Irvine, Author

Wildlife and Conservation Advocate

THE SALON ON THE SPIRITUALLY CREATIVE LIFE, JUNE 2010

"When it comes to wildlife and nature, life is most certainly filled with surprises and unexpected lessons. I've had close encounters with a plethora of furry, feathered and scaly creatures from anteaters to zebras throughout my thirty-two-year communications career at the San Diego Zoo, my work as an author of more than twenty books about animals, and my worldwide travels. But a chance meeting with a rambunctious orangutan in Borneo counts among my most incredible, awe-inspiring experiences.

"I was a new volunteer for the Orangutan Foundation International (OFI), spending my first day out in the nursery forest adjacent to the Orangutan Care Center and Quarantine Facility near Pangkalanbun, Borneo. It was late August 2002 – the dry season – and I had never been so hot and sticky in all my life. My job was to photograph orangutans and write stories about their personalities as well as their plight for OFI's web site and printed materials.

"I was sitting on a log, taking a break from shooting photos in hopes that I would cool down a bit, when I noticed several male orangutans roughhousing on a mound of dirt about ten yards away. One in particular caught my eye, and his distinctive appearance and awkward actions frightened me a bit so I told myself that I should be careful not to get too close to him. His name was Montana, and he was exceptionally large compared to the other young males who were in the forest that day. He was partially paralyzed on one side, so he walked hunched over and with a limp; he was missing an eye; and he had scraggly 'pirate' teeth. And, as the caretakers had told me he was 7 or 8 years old, an age when orangutans can be unpredictable, that added to my apprehension.

Georgeanne comforts Montana

"You can imagine my surprise when, as I was looking down fiddling with my camera, Montana suddenly appeared by my side and gently put his arm around my shoulders and just peered into my eyes. It was almost as if he had sensed my fear and had come up to tell me not to be afraid. We sat there for several moments looking at each other and then he plopped down beside me for a rest.

"After a while, I began pulling some sharp stickers out of my pants and wouldn't you know it – Montana started helping me, pulling out the stickers one by one! His kindness and gentleness touched my heart and I became overwhelmed with emotion. As enormous tears rolled down my cheeks, Montana once again peered into my eyes, touched my tears and gently wiped them from my face. Then he hugged me! It was the most amazing experience in the world and something I will never forget as long as I live. This huge, hulking orangutan was, indeed, a gentle spirit, and his looks and size had most certainly been deceiving.

"Orangutans have feelings and emotions just as we do. They are thinking beings and when you see the devastation that is happening to their forest homes and how they are treated by illegal loggers and poachers, it just breaks your heart. I later learned that Montana's mother had been shot, and his lameness and the loss of his eye occurred during this tragic accident. Fortunately, he was rescued and nursed back to health at the Care Center, where he also saw the kind and loving side of the human race.

"What's especially exciting and heartwarming is that Montana is one of the orangutans that Dr. Birute Galdikas, the founder of OFI and the world's foremost orangutan expert, will soon release into the forests of Lamandau, a protected reserve. Montana is a true survivor and has overcome his disabilities enough to be set free into a world he never should have taken from in the first place.

"Experiences such as this one with Montana nourish my soul, intensify my spirituality, and reinforce my belief that we are interconnected with

all living beings. Yet we now are at a crossroads as we challenge the very survival of our planet and its wildlife with human-made anomalies such as urbanization, habitat destruction, climate change, and non-sustainable use of our resources. Our world is most definitely facing a crisis.

"However, as my dear friend Dr. Jane Goodall often reminds me, we must have hope for the future. She says that if every person takes responsibility and does just a few small good deeds to help heal the earth, Nature is forgiving and, with our nurturing, she will regenerate and flourish."

We all must call on the power of Love and use it now – in the big challenges facing our planet and in the little challenges that face us daily. Acknowledging the power of Love and our ability to let it direct our ways is our *real* estate. While life can seem so fragile, Love is strong enough to replace fear of failure with joyful expectancy, gratitude and kindness. We must simply remember whatever we expect or hope to find in this world we have to cultivate first within ourselves – and all that takes is recognition of our *real* estate and then diligently tending its soil.

On the third Thursdays and Saturdays of every month I open the gates, sunup to sundown, to continue the tradition of artists who for more than a century have been coming to capture on canvas the vistas available from the site where we have built our home. I myself sometimes set up my own easel to study the illumination of Mother Nature's light on flora, fauna and our occasional models.

Early one morning as I was opening up our gates for the monthly gathering of this painting society, William, one of the local *plein air* artists,

arrived. (*Plein air* artists paint while experiencing the landscape rather than in the studio.) "Welcome," I said as I waved him down toward the area under the bridge where the others were parked. "Please come up to the house when you need a break so I can learn more about you."

A little later he did, and, after sharing donuts and coffee together, we walked back to see the sketch he had started of the bridges, the eucalyptus trees and the wildflowers. As we walked toward his easel and the view beyond, he stretched forth his arms as if the magnificence of all creation was stretched before him and exclaimed, "How beautiful!"

"Well, not all beautiful," I thought. William was looking at not only nature's finery silhouetted against the furthest and historic bridge but also unavoidable patches of debris and graffiti in between. I couldn't stop myself from wondering how his praise of the place surrounding him could be so unqualified. So I said, "I am so glad you are here and pleased that you like it, but – what exactly is your definition of beauty?"

Obviously a thoughtful man and not given to short answers, William sat down on one of the boulders at our feet and gestured that I should do the same. There together we sat for some time, taking in the view, bidding "good morning" to a few other artists as they arrived, but otherwise saying nothing. Finally, picking up an aged remnant of fountain grass and holding its thin, dry stalk up to the sun, as if its unplanted seeds and withered stalk were as gorgeous as any necklace of diamonds and gold, he said:

"Beauty, as the sages say, is in the eye of the beholder, and our entire lives can be filled with beauty if we will only see it."

"And how do you see it?" I asked.

"For us to see beauty, we must be sensitive to ourselves. The degree of our own sensitivity to our own inner being determines the beauty we will see.

"Something is beautiful according to the richness of appreciation it yields to the viewer, the degree to which it makes you or me feel alive and sensitive to life.

"Great beauty has to do with the degree to which an object imparts dynamics higher than the object itself. This may have to do with its relationship to other objects and how it is arranged with them, or its color, shape and texture. But it most definitely has to do with memories,

present feelings and aspirations – the references it has to us personally. And most important, it has to do with the kind, loving appreciation we ourselves can accept and express.

"For something is never beautiful in and of itself. Any one thing can be seen as the most beautiful object in the world – or the ugliest! Any one thing can be seen as the most exciting object in the world – or the most boring! And, of course, all this is true also in terms of how we view other people.

"Beauty can be said to have proportion, grace and harmony. But it cannot have any of these attributes without our seeing them – and we cannot see them without our own loving and kind appreciation."

Buddist monk expressing kindness
even to the lice inhabiting his robe.

It may be a long time before we can bring a pure sense of devotion to every task and be governed by kindness totally. Meantime, for inspiration, I like to remember a story about a Buddhist monk. This monk, who had found a peaceful and solitary spot along a gently flowing creek, was meditating on goodness for some time. In fact, he had been doing so for six years. Thus one day when he awoke from his sitting trance-like state, he decided it was probably time for him to wash his long cloth covering. He took it off, and when he did he discovered a large number of lice that had taken up home inside where his body kept the cloth and therefore the lice nice and warm.

Well! That monk proceeded to pick up each of the lice and gently place it on a stone by the creek. The monk then washed his cloak and, after it had dried in the sun, put it on again – and then carefully picked up each of the lice and placed it back inside!

May we all be so kind.

Aldous Huxley's dying wish –
"That we should all be kinder...."

In his Salon presentation, "Stray Musings on a Way to the Way," Dr. Satinder Dhiman, author/teacher of spirituality and leadership, and Associate Dean of the School of Business at Woodbury University, recalled what Aldous Huxley said on his deathbed. He knew he was dying, and, since he had spent his entire life in such deeply contemplative thought that many consider him the greatest intellect of the twentieth century, he was asked by those gathered around, 'What is the most important lesson you have learned?' Aldous Huxley's answer was stunning. "That we should all be kinder, a little bit kinder," he said.

To be kind is the most important thing we can ask of ourselves. In everything we do or say, we can try to be a little kinder. This means not only must the broadly influential actions of political, corporate and other groups be humane, civilized and kind. It means that we as individuals must be kinder in all the little things we do day by day and hour by hour. Kindness must govern the way we cook a meal and place it before a family member or friend, the way we care for our possessions, the way we talk, the way we listen, the way we gaze out upon the world from the moment we awaken until we close our eyes at night. Our own individual thoughts and actions, governed by kindness, are our *real* estate.

YOU AND KINDNESS...

When you take responsibility
to be a little bit kinder,
everything and everyone around you
will regenerate and flourish.

Let kindness govern your thoughts
as well as your actions, and your actions
as well as your thoughts.

Beauty only becomes visible through
your own loving and kind appreciation.

Be open to sharing whatever you have with others.

You can never be lost from your own innate kindness –
your *real* estate.

TALE VII Pavilions of the Mind
HARMONY

Meet me down by the brook,

Sweet Breeze. You know my favorite nook

In the grasses that grow tall by my height's

Rock. Don't go one whisk further, Breeze,

For the water nips its passers-by

Just a foot away and would have

You rushed along with it. But stay

And stir the tall grasses in which I'll stand.

Stir, too, my thoughts. Cut their roots

And let them rise higher than

The grasses can. And let them ride

With you. My dormant thoughts.

PAVILIONS OF THE MIND – HARMONY

If you dwell in your highest thoughts, harmony will be yours. Trying to get as close as I can to this idea, I walk out to the farthest reaches of our property and beyond. So thankful am I that the Arroyo is being preserved for us wanderers, all those in search of drinking in the natural landscape's seasonal assurances that the earth is a blessed eternally rejuvenating space. Amid its vast stretches of tall grasses, whispering sycamores and cottonwoods quenched by rivulets from the San Gabriel Mountains' melting snows, we can seek inspiration through solitude. We sink into our own interior landscape while sensing its connection to the universal.

Through Pasadena's preservation efforts, inroads of contamination are being fought and diminished. The land is being restored to the grace of its past when the Native Americans who lived here found the banks of the Arroyo ideal for their own gentle agrarian living and creative pursuits. After the creek waters are cleansed, it is hoped that the Arroyo chub and even the trout will thrive again here as they did for thousands and thousands of years. What a gift it is to be in the center of a community that understands the fragility of our earthly sphere and that cares enough to nurture its origins and to hold on high the lessons of those who have gone before.

THE FUTURE LIES IN OUR HANDS TODAY

Qingyun Ma, Architect

Dean, School of Architecture, University of Southern California
Founder, MADA s.p.a.m. architectural firm based in Shanghai
Founder, American Academy in China/USC

THE SALON ON THE SPIRITUALLY CREATIVE LIFE, NOVEMBER 2009

Qingyun Ma

"We must constantly seek to be attuned to the essence of life. Regardless of our chosen path, we need to consider the larger context, from one's local community to planet Earth. This is what The Salon on the Spiritually Creative Life asks us to do and what the harmonious environment at Arroyo del Rey represents.

"Speaking as an architect: architecture is an assertive action; it clears a site, removes lives, and constructs new objects and spaces. But, it must be sensitive and reactive at the same time. The sensitivity is through the way it learns from what it replaces, both in space and time. It is reactive, because it engenders lives that extend until the next piece of architecture takes place.

"This very notion of regeneration is the essential role of architecture and should be central to all creative efforts. The residence of the Kings is a perfect place in the understanding and demonstration of this notion."

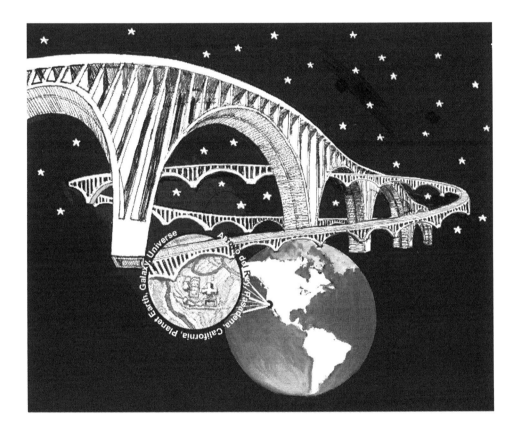

"We need to consider the larger context, from one's local community to planet Earth."

— Qingyun Ma

On this plane of existence, we can ask to feel at one with everything. We can pray for atonement (at-one-ment). We can strive to reveal to ourselves our spiritual essence. We can seek to be part of the essence that is and always has been and always will be. We can consciously fight against the otherwise overwhelming barrage of information based solely on material evidence analyzed through a purely human perspective. Such a narrow viewpoint would have us think of ourselves as primarily physical beings, whereas this is nothing but false testimony regarding Life's true nature.

Feeling at one with everything means living in the moment. Even if we are just washing the dishes, we must be completely present. We must be totally conscious. Give thanks for the meal just completed. Give thanks for the people who shared it. Give thanks for the water that washes the dishes. Give thanks for the dishes. Wash them tenderly, not hurriedly. Keep the harmony. Stay in tune to the nobility of now. And do this for every single aspect of Life.

There is Spirit in the form of everything on earth. This is one of the things I look for when I go walking with Gypsy in the Arroyo. What can

I see afresh today? What can I learn from this tree, this leaf, this rock? Billions of years have gone into making this speck of sand. Billions of years have gone into making me. What new inspiration can I draw from this full, rich heritage? What has been the inherent direction of each individual aspect of life and can I intuit its innate intention?

But soon in my quiet solitary walks, I learn to not even speak to myself as I seek a better understanding. Speech interferes with wisdom. The term "billions of years" does not adequately express infinity. "Making" cannot be equated with eternal perfection. "Want to be" does not do justice to the never-beginning and never-ending nature of Life and Love.

The best way to set myself free in the Arroyo is to set my thoughts free, too. Let my thoughts fly with the wind. Let my thoughts, washed and clean, dance in unfettered harmony with the Spirit of the forms.

CREATING IN HARMONY WITH NATURE

Peter Adams, Artist
President of the California Art Club

THE SALON ON THE SPIRITUALLY CREATIVE LIFE, JANUARY 9, 2000

"An artist and oil painter like myself has a plethora of moods and subject matters that he or she may choose to depict. I believe that the best artwork reflects the handiwork of the Creator and, if the artwork is truly successful, the viewer can sense the hand of God in the work itself. In that way, art can actually be a bridge to the Divine.

"Perhaps for this reason landscape painting in recent years has become very popular. Most people I know today feel there is something god-like in nature, something that is pristine, unspoiled and good. Some actually feel that, by purchasing a work of fine art that expresses the beauty in nature, they are committing an act of reverence.

"The act of painting out of doors is also a very spiritual experience. Being in nature, being surrounded by its grandeur, while concentrating on the shapes of trees, distant mountains and clouds, and trying to render atmospheric effects, tends to humble an artist and tends to calm the soul.

"Perhaps William Wendt, the second president of the California Art Club which was founded in 1909, said it best when he stated: 'The perfection of this spring day and the gladness thereof make one think of Genesis when the earth was young and morning stars sang to each other. The earth is young again. The peace, the harmony which pervades all, gives a Sabbath-like air to the day, to the environment. One feels that he is on holy ground, in Nature's Temple .... The perfumes of the flowers and of the bay tree are wafted on high, like incense .... The birds sing sweet songs to praise their Creator. In the tops of the trees, the soughing of the wind is like the hushed prayers of the multitude in some vast cathedral. Here the heart of the man becomes impressionable. Here, away from the conflicting creeds and sects, away from the soul-destroying hurly-burly of life, it feels that the world is beautiful, that man is his brother, that God is good.'"

Guests lingered a long time after Peter Adams led The Salon that Sunday, for after his presentation he had set up his easel under the bridges and allowed them to continue discussing life and art even as he put oil on canvas. The day was coming to its end and the setting sun etched the San Gabriel Mountains' otherwise purple embrace with rhythmic lines of gold. Being one of my favorite hours to wander down to our gazebo, I asked a few of the attendees, including one named Jacob, to join me there for tea and conversation.

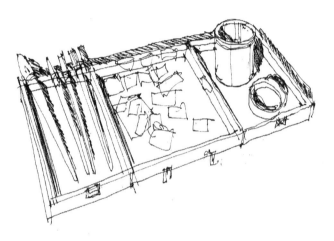

Also an artist for most of his long and respected life as well as a highly advanced yogi, Jacob is one of the most elegant men I have ever known, as elegant as the canvases on which he has left his imprint and thus gained renown. Yet, like the individual aspects of the paintings he has composed, neither his dress nor physical presentation leaves a memorable impression. No, when he departs one's company, one can remember nothing but the loving, radiant glow that seems to linger wherever he walks. We had settled into the gazebo's willow chairs, which my

husband had purchased from a family in Arkansas who also made our love-seat nestled under an oak on a plateau overlooking the gazebo. I explained that I had always been most interested in advancing my understanding of the difference between man-made items which seem only material and other items whose significance seems much greater.

"I write about the arts," I said, "and I have always felt they do empower people's lives, that they are more than skin-deep material things for us to possess. Yet giving expression to their importance without letting the whole subject sound once again as something more material than spiritual is a challenge. I wish so much that you would give it a try."

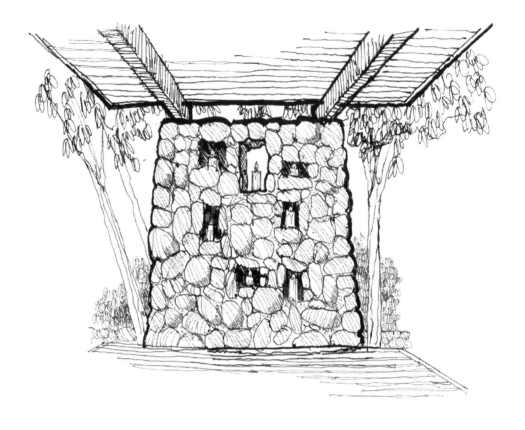

Jacob's response was so slow in coming that the last sun rays started to disappear from the oaks above and the creek below. I rose to light the candles set within the gazebo's one wall, made of river rock and inset with niches. That task done, I settled down again and still his look of reverie went past me as if, instead of thinking of an answer to my question, he was waiting for his own inner being to speak. Finally his visage glowed with much more than the candles' reflection. And when he spoke, it was more like music than speech.

"Your environment, as is your life, is composed not just of what you have been given, rented or bought. It is composed of that which you bring to it of your own intelligence, inventiveness, imagination and, above all else, your inner harmony. The degree to which intelligence, inventiveness and imagination influence everything else is important. Yet the harmony you bring to your environment can be said to be its absolutely most important, highest quality.

"Not to take advantage of this power to influence your life means that, instead of expressing yourself to your full advantage, you are reacting to your surroundings in an unthinking manner – reacting to, instead of lovingly governing and caring for, the space around you.

"But we are not reactors. We are not machines. We are doers. We *are* the power. And because of that, regardless of our occupations, we are all 'artists.' We are all capable of imagining, making decisions and creating. Therefore we must make use of our power to live not only fully but harmoniously.

"We must work to bring a deeply felt sensitivity into every aspect of our lives. We should demand that our lives and our environment be as expressive of love as possible. We should insist that we awaken in ourselves the ability to appreciate and enjoy every moment of our days. Living with care – doing everything throughout the day with care and passion – enhances life. For what is art but organized emotion? The ability to organize emotion positively, not the so-called 'style' of things themselves, is what raises an object or an activity into the realm of art.

"In our lives, we should strive to unify the action with the mood, the sense with the spirit. And all of us do have the capability of achieving this unity, for within each of us lies an artist. Within each of us lies the unending source of art, and that is loving harmony. Loving harmony is the highest form of mindfulness."

As Jacob drove away that day, up and out the steep grade of our driveway, Gypsy and I stood at the top and waved good-bye. Yet long after Jacob's silver-gray vehicle had delivered him from sight, we continued to be caressed by his own example of serene, loving harmony.

STRAY MUSINGS ON A WAY TO THE WAY

Satinder Dhiman, PhD, EdD
Author, Co-founder, Business Renaissance Institute
Associate Dean, School of Business, Woodbury University

THE SALON ON THE SPIRITUALLY CREATIVE LIFE, JUNE 1999

"One of the sweet 'catches' of life is that only hindsight is 20/20. Yet there is a certain inevitability about every event in our life. Everything is exactly the way it should be in the cosmic scheme of things. Zen masters remind us that everything is on schedule in the universe. To wit, life just happens to us amidst our plannings and projections. 'Now' is rightly called 'present' - a 'gift' from gods. The key is to be alertly aware in the present moment, a la Eckhart Tolle. It is a strange realization that even past and future can only be experienced in the now, the eternal present moment.

"As long as there is any aspiration to become something different than what we are, life remains a struggle. By relinquishing the need to be different than what we are, we step out of the cycle of becoming and enter into the peaceful abode of being. Being yourself involves no struggle, it is the most easy and natural thing in life and requires no time. It is always available to us here and now, effortlessly.

"Peace is our natural state - that is why whenever we are not peaceful or harmonious, we want to get back to our natural state. There is nothing one has to do. In fact, anything we do with our volitional mind takes us away from this innate state of our being. In some Indian scriptures, this state has been likened to what is referred to as Sat-Chit-Anand or Being-Consciousness-Bliss, ie, remaining – 'Being' – in our natural state of pure consciousness – 'Awareness' – is the key to peace/bliss. Happiness comes from outside and we have to do something about it. Bliss on the other hand is our natural inner state. We just have to '*be*.'"

YOU AND HARMONY...

Seek to be attuned to the harmonious essence of life.

Match your actions with your sensitivity.

The order, cleanliness and harmony you
maintain will be reflected in all areas of your life.

Even on this earthly plane of existence, you can feel at
one with everything, for you *are* at one with everything.

The harmony which pervades everything in the universe is
yours today and every moment therein.

Loving harmony is the highest form of mindfulness.

Peace is your natural inner state.

TALE VIII The Creek Never Ends
LOVE

Golden hair and shimmering rays
On glistening gems mid our creek's run,
My little girl is lost in play --
By gathering stones, she holds the sun!

Vertical spires of green surround
No man-made object on this spot.
Only my child lost in play,
A child attuned to her soul today.

Hallowed moment, oh sylvan scene
Of daughter entranced by garden's gleam,
Nurturing every future year
By being at one with nature here.

Intimate feelings beyond compare
Of understanding her oneness there
Can help forever the human race -
A child aware of nature's grace!

In understanding the power of Love, we must not focus on anything but the brotherhood of all people. Love connects everyone and everything. We must exercise the highest level of discernment between that which is merely distracting, and Love which is all embracing and empowering.

GIVING WITHOUT RESERVATION

Joan F. Marques, EdD
Author, Co-Founder, Business Renaissance Institute
Professor of Business and Management
Woodbury University

THE SALON ON THE SPIRITUALLY CREATIVE LIFE, AUGUST 2004

"One of my favorite illustrative stories is from an unknown author about a wise woman who was traveling in the mountains and found a precious stone. Shortly thereafter, the wise woman met another traveler who was hungry, so she offered to share her food. But the other traveler saw the precious stone and asked the wise woman to give it to him. She did not hesitate, and gave him the stone. As their ways parted, the traveler was elated, because he was aware that this stone was valuable enough to grant him security for the rest of his life. Yet, the next day he set out to find the wise woman and return the stone. When he found the woman, he said, 'I've been thinking. I know how valuable the stone is, but I give it back in the hope that you can give me something even more precious. Give me what you have within you that enabled you to give me the stone.'

"This story illustrates the magnitude of attitude. It takes a tremendous amount of self-disregard to give away your most valuable asset, but if you can, you have demonstrated a degree of greatness that is hard to attain by many. Shaping our attitude is a lifelong learning process, which we attain through the books we read, the people we meet, and the reflections we breed. It's almost a slippery slope, with progress and regress, but as long as we remain open to learn, wisdom is in sight. In our highly individualistic society we often maintain a 'what's in it for me' mentality – which infringes on our good intentions. We do so, because we cannot see into the future, and therefore don't understand the full essence of giving without reservation. Yet, those of us who have given without holding back have found that the rewards come in unexpected shapes, at unexpected moments, and from unexpected corners."

Following Dr. Marques's Salon presentation, some of us gathered around two of the attendees, a couple who had just celebrated their seventieth wedding anniversary. In these days of quick marriage and easy divorce, we were eager to glean some wisdom from this 96-year-old man and his 92-year-old wife who had found the secret for staying together, evidently happily, for seven decades. Bob and Sonia, however, had never given a thought to the possibility that their marriage might be anything but forever.

"We came from loving homes, homes in which love was number one. We didn't believe in divorce, and there was none in our families," Bob said. "We pledged that we would stay together 'til death do us part, and that's the only way it could have been."

Sonia admitted that problems do arise even in the happiest marriage. "I've never known anyone who could truthfully say he or she had been married for even five years and not had problems. In fact, you wouldn't want not to have them," she said. "Problems serve to bring you and your spouse closer together. After the struggle of raising a family and putting the children through school, we grew closer. And now that the strain of life is over, we grow closer every day. We know that life is short, and we want to make the most of it."

Since they had retired, they were just reveling in going to bed at the same time, arising together every morning at seven o'clock and enjoying their meals together. In fact, it had been many years since they had not been able to be together almost every hour of each day. Yet they never tired of their closeness. They relished it.

"You know," said Sonia as she reclined comfortably on our sofa beside her husband, "I'm never quite so happy as when he is sitting right here beside me. I want him *close* to me."

But what did they do when one did something the other didn't like? Did she get angry? Did he hold resentment inside of him, to let it come out later in some snide remark?

"I believe we just forgot it," Bob said.

"You know, I'm the naughty one," Sonia added. "I've said nasty things. But it's never three minutes before he'll come back with something funny or sweet. He'll do it every time.

"And although I don't pop back quite as quickly as he does, I'm sort of the same way. We just forget it. That's all you need to do."

Bob agreed, "The sense of humor has been the outstanding thing in our lives." Then he told a story, an anecdote from their lives together, and she laughed as if she had never heard it before.

Then, with her husband listening as attentively as if they were just getting to know one another, Sonia told of one problem she had had which many women would not have gotten over.

"The most difficult experience I've ever had and the one that hurt me the most was when my husband joined the army as a chaplain in World War II. I was three-months pregnant and I felt he could get out of going overseas with the military, but he wanted that adventure.

"Well, at that time the flu epidemic was killing so many pregnant women, and I had two older children to raise, I just couldn't understand how he could leave me."

So how did she forgive him, we asked?

"The joy of our baby boy, the joy of having my husband come home again," Sonia replied. "It's the joy that overcomes all bad feelings. And you can forget so easily, if you just let Love flow."

UNCONDITIONAL LOVE AND KINDNESS IN TROUBLED TIMES

The Venerable
Tulku Karma Gyurme Sonam Rinpoche
[known as Tulku Tsori Rinpoche]

SALON ON THE SPIRITUALLY CREATIVE LIFE, FEBRUARY 2009

Recognized as a Lama, a term reserved for senior members of the Tibetan Order, Rinpoche is founder and spiritual leader of the Yogi Tsoru Dechen Foundation based in Miami, Florida. The foundation was created to provide Westerners access to the Buddha Dharma [Path of Awakening] and to supply compassion and wisdom to all human beings. Yet as Rinpoche continues to devote his life to champion humanitarian efforts, one cannot help but wonder: after the harsh experiences of his own personal history, how he can be so open, selfless and giving?

Rinpoche was born in Nepal in 1974. At the age of 3, he was recognized as a "Tulku," one who intentionally reincarnates for countless lifetimes to offer the Buddha's teachings. Rinpoche is recognized and blessed by His Holiness the Dalai Lama and has received teachings from many of the great Tibetan masters.

Yet when Tulku, as his followers now call him, was only 8-years old, the political strife between China and Tibet disrupted the harmony of the outward appearances of his auspicious beginnings. He was lost from his parents and was sold into servitude, a situation that continued until he was 15 and during which he was considered no more than a piece of merchandise. Once he was even traded for a German Shepherd dog.

On that day of the Salon, a time of much political, financial and ethical turmoil in many corners of the world including our own United States, there could have been no one more important from whom to hear. Tulku had spoken to those gathered at the Salon for an hour or so – speaking of the kind of total Love we usually have for our mothers, "our mothers who gave us everything, even our life itself." And then he said we should focus on expressing that kind of total Love to every other thing, every other being, every insect. "In such a way we should pay homage to every thing and every being in the universe. We should realize that the other being – even if it is a bug we find under a rock – could be our mother, *is* the same as our mother. It is this kind of unconditional Love we need to practice," he said.

Tulku conveyed his message with such quiet yet strong certainty, and with such effusive yet gentle Love, that it was with some hesitation that I at last asked my question: "Tulku, there are so many aspects of life that would seek to disquiet us. Right here in this room are those who have loved ones who are facing terminal illnesses. Others are facing the loss of their home due to dishonesty of those entrusted with their life savings. Others have lost family members to the Holocaust. You yourself went through great emotional and physical hardship – not to mention what this must have done to your own mother and father. In the face of such catastrophes, how is it possible still to nurture the discipline of Love and kindness?"

Tulku looked at me and, with the most courteous demeanor, appeared to ponder my question for several moments. Yet, even before I asked the question, I knew he had answered it for himself countless times before and in a way completely freeing him from any sense of anger or loss or regret. His understanding enables him to place himself within an impenetrable sanctuary where bitterness and concern not only cannot enter but where they are seen to not even exist.

"We simply have to understand the passing nature of everything," he said, opening his arms wide to indicate everything before us that we could see and everything beyond our vision as well. "All of this in our material world – absolutely all of it! – is ephemeral. It is nothing! The only thing that matters is Love – our understanding of Love and our expression of Love."

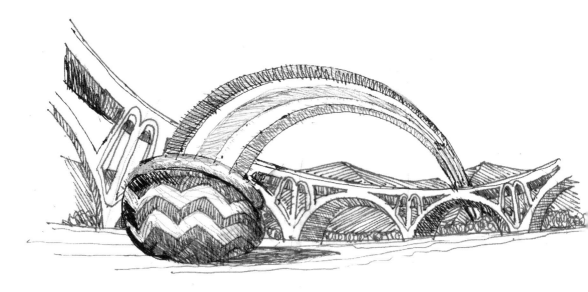

Later that day, as our guests were leaving, the air seemed filled with glorious, jubilant thoughts ... thoughts that can inspire, and also heal.

Such is often the feeling following the Salons – each person finding a new personal vision whereby the mundane becomes enchantment. On this day, the speaker Tulku had offered a glimpse of perfect, harmonious Love, and to us it seemed like ambrosia of the highest truth. It energized us as we each individually could reflect and go forward, taking with us what seemed most appropriate for our own personal lives.

It is right for each of us to find our own way to seek truth. We do not need to wait for the right teacher, church or temple. The truth lies within each one of us, and we can start to discover it today.

I am always thankful for such gifts of inspiration, for even during my years with Richard at our cherished home, things have not all been wonderful. Some such things are easier to deal with than others. I have learned that the end of a business venture can seem tragic, but it can also lead to better things – and even before the darkness disappears, one must trust that the sun will shine again and work toward that end. Having a loved one turn away can cause actual physical pain in the heart ... heartsick is not just a symbolic word to one who has felt its anguish. And the worst part about it is that, when no understanding is available to soothe it, it can turn to a bitterness that could eat through one's other relationships and even one's attitude toward life. The only thing one can do is to set Love free without malice, to let it fly with the wind and bid it well. At a recent Salon, author/futurist Ray Bradbury put it this way, "Go for the Love! Don't wait! Jump off the cliff for it – build your wings on the way down!"

An understanding of the inseparable connection between Life and Love and man can lead to the realization of our perfection. The only reality is Love and Life. When fully understood, life on earth becomes imbued with a light that takes away the shadows. Even the negativity associated with aging is erased, and each day is seen as a more full and complete stage of understanding. Then, when the body ceases to be of service, or when it is time for an individual to leave this earthly sphere, his or her real identity is not only undiminished but even more fully illuminated than before. Experiencing this transition with a loved one provides a clear demonstration that, truly, the creek never ends.

YOU AND LOVE…

You must understand the full essence
of giving without reservation.

Weed out all negativity and bitterness
and replace them with Love.

If you let Love flow, you can forgive anything.

The only thing that matters is Love –
your understanding of Love and your expression of Love.

Try loving your loved one's imperfections!

Let Love illuminate your perceptions,
including the way you view your age, your
abilities, and your abundance.

TALE IX Empowered Places
HEALING

Riding a stallion are we!
Without restraints, life runs wild.
Without a groom, life loses the race.
Riding a stallion are we!

So let discipline be our standard,
Peace and order be our reins.
Whip lightning fast 'yond fear, greed, envy –
And homeward speed to the girth of Love.

Riding a stallion are we!
Let ours be the one guided by Love!

How can we maintain our positive attitude when poverty, sickness, death and other misfortunes seem at highest tide? Two of my friends did so in ways that continue to make a huge and positive difference in the lives of others. Following is an abbreviation of their personal journeys which they shared at The Salon.

TURNING CHALLENGE INTO OPPORTUNITY

Valerie von Sobel
Founder, Andre Sobel River of Life Foundation

Alyce Morris Winston
Founder, The Jeffrey Foundation

THE SALON ON THE SPIRITUALLY CREATIVE LIFE, JUNE 2005

Just one decade before this Salon, Valerie von Sobel's 18-year-old son, Andre, a fine athlete, had felt dizzy. The doctor discovered an incurable tumor. Andre died soon after. Valerie's husband, a highly successful attorney, had not been able to face the anniversary of his son's passing. So Valerie's husband, fueled by depression and medicines that sent his will to live spiraling downwards, took his own life. Thus Valerie needed to face the loss of two loved ones alone. How can one possibly handle such crises?

In the end, after a period of meditating and healing, Valerie turned her own anguish into positive, powerful energy. Soon after, she felt led to create the Andre Sobel River of Life Foundation to help parents of

children with incurable diseases. As she had learned during Andre's many hospitalizations, not all parents are as fortunate as she was in being able to provide for a family's shelter and food when one child needs round-the-clock attention, not to mention expensive medical care.

Similar to Valerie in forcing her grief to make an about-face is Alyce Morris Winston. Her adopted son, Jeffrey, had multiple sclerosis and she cared for him unfailingly. Her husband, unwilling or unable to continue with the demands of the situation, left home never to return, and Alyce found that she could not care for her son and also work. To make ends meet, she took in others' children who needed constant physical and emotional care – washing their clothes and giving them playtime and nap time right along with Jeffrey. When a teenager, Jeffrey passed away, but Alyce, who by now had discovered her life's mission, founded The Jeffrey Foundation to continue to provide the daily physical care and educational support of special needs children of working parents.

Since many of these parents are single mothers, they are in the exactly same position in which Alyce had found herself decades before – which, of course, is one reason for her infinitely understanding presence among them today. Just to be around Alyce is to experience a degree of healing.

During The Salon, both Alyce and Valerie spoke about the surprise of finding that even their darkest hours were finally banished with a light of healing clarity. Neither of them ever realized that she possessed such a deep well of inner strength. Looking back on how they were able to draw from that treasured source, Valerie said she believes it was her use of prayer and meditation. Alyce credited her ability to "just keep going," and also now to have a most supportive husband, Edgar Winston, always at her side. In addition both Valerie and Alyce emphasized how important it had been to find delight in all the little daily joys, no matter how small, and concentrating on their gratitude for Life -- not allowing forms of sickness to get them down, but instead opening their hearts to Life's wondrous beauty. And they both adored their precious sons beyond imagining.

It is evident that Valerie and Alyce both have achieved an almost childlike sense of life. Despite all the physical evidence to the contrary, they have opened their vision to Life's original, unsullied purity and allowed Love, completely unblemished by disappointment and bitterness, to flourish. As they have responded to the needs of mothers and their children in circumstances similar to their own, they have inspired countless others by the way they have turned adversity into a positive force for good.

None of us can ignore the immense suffering and destruction that fear and ignorance have allowed to take hold on our beautiful planet earth. Yet all of us, as exemplified by Valerie von Sobel and Alyce Morris Winston, *can* do something. The feeling of helplessness is but an excuse for laziness.

Richard at his favorite place for quiet thinking

I like to recall the words of writer/intellectual William F. Buckley, "Despair is a mortal sin." Another inspirational voice is author Norman Cousins, reminding us how panic, fear and rage contribute to the belief in seemingly disastrous circumstances including disease, while hope, faith, Love and laughter can preserve our health and well-being. These were his tools when he was diagnosed with an "incurable" illness. And he recovered.

We can all fight for "recovery," and the first place to start is in our own home. We can be less wasteful and more productive. We can eliminate bitterness and anger and we can be more understanding. And, as did Norman Cousins, we all can uplift our attitudes and even bring physical healing into our lives with hope, faith, Love and laughter.

Our home is the first place to purify and the first place sunup to sundown and throughout the night to raise our consciousness with our best thoughts. Our home is the one place we can somewhat control, even if it is just to establish one corner and one period of time to meditate in peace and on peace.

We also can meditate outside in nature, in addition to our home the most nurturing place for most of us while we are here on earth. Richard's favorite place for quiet thinking is our chair hidden behind some oleanders. Its rustic shape made of abandoned farm implements constantly beckons him to sit down and relax. He looks out over the creek and the trail where an occasional jogger or rider on horseback enlivens the view. And he devotes himself to healing contemplation.

I most often retreat to the Pavilion which has become my studio, or I will take paper and pen down to the Gazebo or out to the stone wall that overlooks one of the most charmingly winding sections of the creek. Then again, every day we bring some offering of nature inside, be it only one exquisite flower or leaf, to help launch our meditative journey by contemplating perfection. And long ago we found we were using our time while gardening and doing other non-mentally-demanding chores as our special private periods of meditation. If we concentrate optimistically and faithfully, even the most mundane of tasks can lead us into a rarified state of consciousness.

We all can think of this time for ourselves as our own special island protected by a walled fortress and surrounded by a moat. Peace, Love and healing Truth will come to surround us there. We do not need to invent them. Of their own accord they will come. That is because they are always with us, our guardian angels that always have been and always will be. We do not have to call them. They are here. We just need to be receptive to the healing and loving wisdom that is a never ending, gently flowing well within each one of us.

At these times, we can mentally contradict every ugly thought. We can adhere to positive thoughts about whomever and whatever come into our experience. We can insist on an uplifted mental picture of them, and infuse our image of them with expectant joy. And those moments of meditation will become our way of being every day of our lives.

In my own life, at the stage when that old bitterness at the seeming tragedies of life could start to grow, I have become able to rid myself of that acidic prey fairly quickly. One of the events that helped prepare me was the loss of my brother on earth.

My brother, Commander Philip Merrill Soucek, a fine, decorated Navy pilot, "lost" his life during a nighttime mission. I intentionally place quotation marks around "lost" because I know that no life is ever really lost. However, when his plane went down, I had been angry, bitterly angry, at everything in the universe.

Almost immediately, I set to work on my thinking. I had to get over that bitterness as quickly as I could so that I could focus on my understanding of the Truth about my brother – that his expression of Love could never die, that his essence remained untouched. I still continue to work on my understanding, for the healing process over the loss of a loved one is fragile and requires constant care and unending vigilance. However, as I said, I now can replace, almost immediately and sometimes in an instant, any erroneous, negative thought with the positive reality of Love.

Of course, attaining completely healed thought sometimes can seem impossible, and at times is not even desired. How would you feel if you had lived the last sixty years with tattooed numbers, the Nazi stamp, on your arm? You might choose to wear long-sleeved clothes for the rest of your life – not to hide any shame, for you would be proud that your people had survived the Holocaust – but just to be free at times of dark memories that would so often cloud every thought. Yet you might also want to never forget.

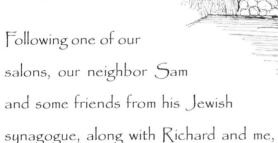

Following one of our salons, our neighbor Sam and some friends from his Jewish synagogue, along with Richard and me, decided to gather down by the creek in the Gazebo, which by now we had nicknamed "The Sanctuary" in honor of the birds and many other beings who have sought peaceful refuge there. The feeling of that quiet haven, with its willow chairs and river rock wall illuminated by candle-filled niches, seemed particularly appropriate for Sam and his friends that day.

As their stories unfolded, it was clear that nearly all of them were really never children. The Nazis stole their youth, disregarded their flesh and life, and taught them their first lesson in life – that man is the only animal which, if completely misled and totally unaware of the Love within, kills for the sake of killing.

So, if you were a Jew who had experienced the Holocaust, retrospection superimposed on thoughts of the future would be evident during your temple's every gathering. You too might remember the systematic liquidation of, perhaps, your mother, father, sisters, brothers and friends. You too might remember those soldiers, soldiers from a country you used to call home, setting your house on fire.

One might have asked, "Is it not futile to remember now how their own homeland could turn against them?" But Sam answered, "No. Memories enable us – and our children – to keep bright our support of Israel."

One man recalled how he and the girl he was to marry were both teenagers when they were sent from Lodz to Auschwitz where parents, brothers and sisters of both were sent only to die. They can remember the very day they became their families' sole survivors.

Together in peace as well as in strife, they married in Sweden before coming to the United States, and they rebuilt their lives. They learned English from television as they entered their trade. By the time of our meeting, they owned a carpet company. Their daughter has never known a land not free.

"Perhaps because of our experience, we're more serious," commented her father. "People say we

Jews are very aggressive. But we've had to be to make up for what we lost. And we have a great fear that we and our children might become complacent, lest the same thing happen again."

"By our vigilance, may we exchange injustice for peace," added his wife. "By our vigilance, may we be healed."

EMPOWERED PLACES

Carol Soucek King, MFA, PhD

The Salon on the Spiritually Creative Life, December 2009

"Admittedly, situations on earth can be incredibly difficult, horrendous beyond imagining. There is no easy fix. But I do know this:

"Wherever we are on this planet earth, whomever we are with and whatever has been done to us, we do have the power to heal our wounds, advance our understanding, and express and experience harmony. And the number one place to start is our home. First is our home *within* - being at home with ourselves, knowing that no one and no event can rob us of our inner Truth and universally-connected, never-ending identity. Second is our physical home.

"What we create in our personal environment and the spirit with which we create it become our daily affirmation of who we are and who we want to be. In Richard's and my own experience, we were fortunate that our architects Conrad Buff III and Don Hensman envisioned, as do we, that a home can serve as a metaphor for all of life. Therefore they understood that maintaining harmony during every moment of creating our home was as important as proportion, balance and line in imparting an uplifting and healing sense of calm. As challenging as the construction process at times must have been, they kept the feeling of peace and joy flowing – as well as plenty of fun, including a laughter-in-the-rafters party! Not surprisingly, after move-in day when Conrad and Don turned on the lights and gave us the key, the positive vibrations of our home continued.

"That is the reason Richard and I always have said, 'Conrad and Don didn't make blueprints for houses. They made blueprints for *living!*'

"They knew that the most important ingredient of a home is not material but spiritual. A home is a never-ending prayer! With appropriate perspective, the seemingly mundane can *always* become enchantment. We simply need to cultivate a sense of awe. We simply need to tune in. And when this is understood, the result can be inspirational, restorative, and even physically healing.

"There is no easy fix for the tempests around us. Yet we can empower our own home, and then our home - whether small or large, humble or grand - can return the favor by sustaining and empowering us."

YOU AND HEALING...

Be receptive to the healing
and loving wisdom that is a never ending,
gently flowing well within each of us.

Replace any erroneous, negative thought
with the positive and healing reality of
kindness, understanding and Love.

When we understand that we are not material
but spiritual beings, the result can be inspirational,
restorative and even physically healing.

Give yourself some alone time each day.
Listen to your inner thoughts.
Meditate. Pray. Focus on wellness.
Concentrate on perfection.

Love heals.

TALE X Sanctuary
SPIRITUALITY

Autumn day, come back, come back,
So I may catch one more colored
Leaf or let down one more curl
For the wind to play with.

It is not enough that I should have
From morn to night to enjoy thee.
I could gaze upon thee forever.
Thy beauty should be eternal.

Must even your brilliance, surely divine,
Grow dim, as all, with the passing of time?
With the fall of night, your brilliant self
Is ushered away to some secret place.

But if I stand and hold my breath
I feel your Love still rustling here.

Down in the Arroyo, two white butterflies seem to be dancing to the symphonic rhapsodies of birds, toads and crickets. As Gypsy and I draw closer to the midst of this orchestra, nature's embrace caresses my total being. Without the computer, telephone and other accoutrements of our modern daily life, we experience with greater clarity and with a richer insight the all-encompassing nature of our true identity. No wonder that the relaxed state of such a walk sets me free to dwell in rapture. And I can see ever more clearly that all energy comes not from the body but from a spiritual interconnectedness with everything and every other being. In this particular setting, it is the Spirit of the many who have come before and set their own creative energies free that continues to inform every breath, every tree, every leaf.

I turn around and look up at our home, this truly magical gift bestowed on us by Conrad and Don, and I am dazzled by the vision of what the "Spirit of the Forms," about which I have often written, truly means. Each harmonious aspect of line, proportion, perspective, light and shadow in the landscape and structure plays a part in a visual symphony. And that symphony reflects what was in their souls and ours as together we unleashed our highest dreams, our humblest odes. We were creating a picture of what we felt in our collective Spirit. We were blessed and that blessing continues. It continues as much in Spirit as in form – and that is what "The Spirit of the Forms" is all about. It is not the spirit of the place by itself but the whole history of people bringing Spirit to what they express. This is enlightened expression, and it sheds its illumination on our sense of place and makes it sacred.

THE UBIQUITOUS COMPUTER

Yoshito "Super" Yamaguchi
Chairman of Sennet, Inc. which produces TRON computer software, the subject of Mr. Yamaguchi's book *Tron*.
Inspirational Leader in Business, Education & Music

THE SALON ON THE SPIRITUALLY CREATIVE LIFE, AUGUST 2008

"Well, at first I have to start with a story from a movie. Do you remember the movie '2001: A Space Odyssey'? This movie is based on a science fiction novel by Arthur C. Clark. The film was directed and produced by Stanley Kubrick and was first released in April 1968, more than forty years ago. The story deals with themes of human evolution, technology, artificial intelligence, and extraterrestrial life. The computer installed in the spacecraft is named HAL, which is an acronym produced from one letter alphabetically ahead of each of the letters in 'IBM.' HAL develops self-consciousness and leads human beings in the new age of evolution. But at the story's end, HAL initiates a mutiny and causes the death of the entire crew, except one.

"The movie shocked many people at that time. The movie also became famous for its theme music derived from Richard Strauss's 'Thus Spoke Zarathustra' (based on Nietzsche). It reflected the mood of the time very well. IBM was then the world's computer giant, and some people truly believed the computer might actually exceed a human being's intelligence and come close to being God.

"Now everyone knows that a computer is a computer and it is obvious that the computer cannot rise above humans to dominate the world. But let me examine the reason for this - the reason that computer systems absolutely cannot evolve to be an entity superior to human beings.

"In order to examine this, let us compare the capability of a computer to a human brain, category by category:

1. Memory capacity
2. Speed of transaction
3. Surmising power
4. Abstraction power
5. Believing power

"In <u>capacity of memory</u>, the computer may surpass the human being. In <u>speed</u>, if the computer is given a simple problem or pattern to solve, it is faster than a human. But for complicated functions, the human being has the upper hand.

"As for <u>surmising power</u>, the computer can surmise but this becomes very difficult.

"And for <u>abstraction power</u>, the computer can learn this but cannot come close to human abstraction capability.

"Finally, as far as <u>belief</u> is concerned, this is completely foreign to the computer. And unlike abstraction power, it is not possible for the computer to learn how to believe.

"Knowing God, or whatever you call the universal supreme being, is the sole major difference between a human and any machine. By knowing God, the human being can establish 'self' and organize himself or herself under a certain spiritual discipline by which we can live our lives. It is this spirituality that is our most important strength."

When first arriving at our home for The Salon on the Spiritually Creative Life, many people have remarked, "This is a spiritual place, have you noticed?" And Richard and I smile. The centuries of peoples harmoniously working together on this land through the arts and crafts and agriculture – centuries of affirming peace and harmony and beauty – have created an atmosphere here that is much more than the individual aspects of flora and fauna.

That atmospheric essence sings to me every day of the importance

of the arts and the humanities in intercultural and international understanding. Not war, not power, not politics, but the arts and all endeavors concerned with civility of thought and relationships and kindness in every aspect of living are the vital ingredients for living. We all must recognize, as far as we are able, the universal Truth and Spirit and let this lead our thoughts and actions. We must recognize our abilities and therefore our responsibility when consciously directing or reflecting present thought or action. To merely react to the appearance of the worldly situation, or to present a dismal picture without expression of faith that it can be restored to a harmonious expression of good, is not fulfilling this responsibility. We must see clearly the present and envision the future in enlightened terms harmonious with the universal wellspring of Spirit and Love that resides within each of us and is yearning for affirmation.

DANCING THE COSMOS INTO CREATION: SHIVA NATARAJA & HINDU SPIRITUALITY

Ingrid Aall, PhD
Author and Proponent for Multi-Cultural Visual Literacy
California State University, Long Beach

THE SALON ON THE SPIRITUALLY CREATIVE LIFE, JANUARY 2010

"How does the artist know what to create?" Dr. Ingrid Aall posed the question within the context of traditional religious Hindu art and proceeded to connect her answer to ageless truths that are universal to the never-ending miracle of the spiritually creative life. "In traditional religious Hindu art, the themes depicted had to be spiritually uplifting. For that reason, since each of their many gods was immortal, unchangeable and eternal, gods were represented in the image of an ideal figure, saturated with life, health and beauty. Exemplifying this are the many depictions of Shiva Nataraja dancing the cosmos into creation.

"Similarly, from ancient times to the present, all artists submit to their respective cultural traditions and in that context creativity is both ageless and truly universal to the never-ending miracle of the spiritually creative life. We would understand this miracle if we knew the answer to: What is inspiration and what is wisdom?

"The two are intertwined. Wisdom has but needs no words - wisdom goes beyond words. Inspiration is knowing what to do when one cannot be wise. Inspiration is the language of the heart, born of Love. Love itself becomes the convener of wisdom manifest in deeds, even if only in a silent smile. Wisdom happens after years of accumulated Love of lived life, as when an experience in life-affirmation bursts into an inspirational overflow."

During the holidays, Richard and I always ask our dinner guests to share a reading, a poem, or scripture that represents to them "uplifted consciousness" – an appropriate term since our friends represent a variety of faiths and paths in their search for enlightenment.

These readings have been our way of making sure that the holidays do not become a time of presents and feasting without our paying homage to the spiritual nature of the event. We hope that, even as we line up for the buffet dinner, our thoughts and conversation will be elevated above mere gossip or newspaper headlines.

I particularly like to recall one such special evening. Arroyo del Rey was laden with paper origami cranes from Japan, symbolically wishing thousands of years of life for everyone. The table was set in Native American-inspired attire, its clay candelabrum illuminating clusters of fountain grass and papier-mâché coyotes. The wreath was of brilliant Mexican paper flowers. Richard set the logs in the fireplace ablaze. Gypsy took his usual central position in our midst.

"First Romus," said Richard, indicating that the first speaker should be my father, whose own father, an immigrant to Oklahoma from Bohemia, had named his four sons after the gods in Greek and Roman mythology or derivatives of their names – Apollo, Zeus, Ormus and Romus. To each of them, brought up in Oklahoma after the nineteenth-century land rush and together making the most of intense hardship, he imparted his understanding of sensitivity, wisdom, Love and patriotism.

Thus it was that a man named Romus Soucek was reading a poem by Henry Wadsworth Longfellow:

> I shot an arrow into the air,
> It fell to earth, I knew not where;
> For so swiftly it flew, the sight
> Could not follow it in its flight.
> I breathed a song into the air,
> It fell to earth, I knew not where;
> For who has sight so keen and strong,
> That it can follow the flight of song?
> Long, long afterward, in an oak
> I found the arrow, still unbroke;
> And the song, from beginning to end,
> I found again in the heart of a friend.

Following Dad, Mother recited her favorite poem, "The Owl and the Pussycat" by Edward Lear. And Dr. Rozella Knox shared the blessing she felt in connection with a patient's recent healing. As she was long revered for doing in her pracitce of family medicine, she had helped restore not only his physical but also his spiritual well-being.

Then Richard called on our great friend, the classical guitarist Liona Boyd. This evening, instead of playing her guitar, she chose to share an ode she had written about music being the international language, as all that music requires of us is to feel and listen with our hearts.

Next to take his turn was Don Hensman, whose architectural partner Conrad Buff III had recently passed away. Don stood in front of the still burning logs, then opened a book he had brought, *A Victorian Posy*, and read aloud "To a Daisy" by James Montgomery, 1771-1854. Its lines are poignantly evocative of our never-ending relationship with our home's fine architects whose simple but sensitive design enabled the life of which Richard and I had dreamed to gently blossom.

> There is a flower, a little flower
> With silver crest and golden eye,
> That welcomes every changing hour,
> And weathers every sky.
> Within the garden's cultured round
> It shares the sweet carnation's bed,
> And blooms on consecrated ground
> In honor of the dead.
> On waste and woodland, rock and plain,
> Its humble buds unheeded rise;
> The rose has but a summer reign,
> The daisy never dies!

After Don closed his book, he stepped outside beyond the fireplace to the porch and came back with something he had hidden there earlier – four potted daisy plants.

Conrad   Don   Carol   Richard

Putting each daisy plant down in sequence, he said, "This is Conrad, this is me, this is Carol, and this is Richard. Tomorrow plant them and let them grow in sunshine forever!"

Hours later, dinner was over, the logs in the fireplace were now just burning embers, and Gypsy was asleep on the window seat. The rest of us remained, quiet but happily fulfilled, gathered around the still cozy hearth. So many truths seemed to hover there. So many hopes for a better world – a better us.

"Now it is your turn," I said to Richard. "Please recite your Native American prayer." So Richard led us outside under the stars, beyond the pool and just in front of the old river rock wall overlooking the Arroyo. Then, as he does at the end of each of the Salons, Richard asked us all to hold hands and repeat after him the oath which Richard first learned from our Native American friends.

"Do all the good you can,

With all the means you can,

In all the ways you can,

To all the people you can,

As long as you can."

YOU AND SPIRITUALITY...

See the present and envision the future
in enlightened terms harmonious with the
universal wellspring of Spirit.

Let the language of the heart
be your spiritual guide.

Allow your spiritual life to provide
a never-ending source of your creativity.

Turn every moment into a treasure
by thinking consistently on a spiritual level.

Affirm to yourself constantly
your true identity as a spiritual being.

Share with others any understanding
of spirituality you have gained.

Do all the good you can as long as you can.

AFTERWORD

for Richard –

There was some ivy and I cut it,

But it continues still to grow.

There was a day and I did live it,

But its sun still golden glows.

There was a fire and we lit it

A long, long time ago,

But it too stays on burning bright,

Because I keep on loving you so.

CREATE YOUR OWN SALON

How I Began The Salon on the Spiritually Creative Life

In my own life, one of the most satisfying things I have ever done was launching The Salon on the Spiritually Creative Life in December 1996. It is a multi-cultural gathering for the expression of positive uplifted thought, and its devotional purpose led to the decision to schedule The Salon on Sunday mornings at our home. On the second Sunday of each month [except that I do not hold The Salon in April, May or December], we meet at 9:30 a.m. when Richard and I offer a buffet of coffee, juice, muffins and fruit, to which some attendees add other treats. From 10 a.m. until noon we concentrate on the presentation/discussion. The subjects have ranged from religion and philosophy to the arts, business and management leadership.... The primary aspect is that the meetings offer not just intellectual exchanges but inspirational mornings intended to lead us toward a higher realm of understanding.

On that Sunday in December 1996 which turned out to be the first meeting of The Salon on the Spiritually Creative Life, we had just four people gathered. Besides Richard and me, they included our architect Don Hensman; he had just taken us to see the new project he was building and we were gathered in our living room afterwards, talking about the importance of positive, uplifted thought guiding architecture or anything with which one is involved. I said, "This is just like the type of salon I have always dreamed of having." "So why don't you do it?" he asked. "Because then I would have to commit myself," I replied. "So commit yourself!" my dear friend Don commanded. Also present was art consultant Beatrix Jakots Barker, who agreed to help me for the first few months, acting as sounding board for my ideas and also suggesting a couple of the early speakers. Soon the group extended to fifty, sometimes seventy people. I have not wished for The Salon to grow further, as our living room where we meet can hold just so many! However, over the years, whenever people ask to be added to the list, I welcome them and it always works out, as not everyone comes to each salon. Indeed, the list has now grown to several hundred people, but I find that a core group comes regularly and others attend infrequently, so there never seem to be too many.

Communicating to this large a number has become a task, but I accept it gladly. It is less a burden than a joy, for The Salon not only has seemed to mean a great deal to other people but also it contributes much depth and purpose to the activities of our family and to the feelings of spirituality in our home. In addition, I have commenced preparing the notice just three times a year – announcing the speakers and subjects for three months at a time, thereby cutting down considerably on the mailings.

I decided from the first to not charge a fee for The Salon or to pay the speakers. I tell the speakers this when first I contact them so that those who agree to give a presentation understand they are doing so as supporters of the idea of The Salon.

For me, finding the audience has worked out naturally, from those first friends who shared an interest, to others who would hear about The Salon and wished to be included. It has all been by word of mouth – conversations with neighbors, friends and family and those in other groups to which I belong. Attendees range from artists, doctors, teachers, students, lawyers, anthropologists, homemakers, businessmen, writers ... and both men and women attend in equal numbers. Of course, if one lives in an apartment or condominium, a notice on the bulletin board might be helpful in starting to form your group. Or a notice could be circulated to those at work, school, classes, and other meetings.

The speakers have been primarily personal acquaintances. Many have been at the top of their fields, but virtually everyone interested in attending such a salon would make a viable speaker as well. Everyone on earth has so much to say, meaningful stories to tell, so much inspiration to impart! In fact, one Sunday when the intended speaker called to say she had broken her leg climbing Mount Kilimanjaro and could not be here, we had to improvise with various attendees who wished to share their own inspirational thoughts or life-uplifting experiences. It turned out to be one of our best meetings ever. Actually, as on that first day when just four of us were gathered discussing thoughts and aspirations, The Salon could always be just that – no designated speaker, just a gathering for contemplative conversation and luminous thought!

ACKNOWLEDGMENTS

My deepest appreciation is given forever to the many people who have infused The Salon on the Spiritually Creative Life with their inspirational presentations and discussions.

And my gratitude is unending for the architects of our home, Conrad Buff III, FAIA, and Donald C. Hensman, FAIA, for creating this haven – our "Arroyo del Rey" under the bridges spanning Pasadena, California's Arroyo Seco. That gratitude continues many-fold for the ongoing guidance of: Conrad and Don's esteemed associate Dennis Smith who continues the firm today as Buff, Smith & Hensman; Don's nephew, the fine woodworker and cabinet maker Mark Traughber; and landscape contractor Tom Oshiyama, son of Howard Oshiyama who first worked with Buff & Hensman to create our gardens, joined now by his son Kyle Oshiyama, partner, Oshiyama Landscape Company. All have played major parts in what has become The Salon's perfect gathering place.

Another blessing for which we are grateful beyond measure is that we will be able to know that our home and meetings such as The Salon and Richard's Business Renaissance Institute and the Buff & Hensman Lectureship will be able to continue for future generations. The School of Architecture/University of Southern California, from which Conrad and Don graduated and where they taught, has agreed to accept our future gift of our house and maintenance endowment.

Under the guidance of the USC School of Architecture's Dean Qingyun Ma and Executive Director of Development Dottie O'Carroll, it has been arranged that Arroyo del Rey will continue in perpetuity as the Carol Soucek King and Richard King Center for Architecture, Arts and the Humanities/USC.

During the same period that the agreement with USC was being completed, the Pasadena City Council met in March 2009 and designated our home as a Historic Monument, a further commitment to protect our home for future generations.

For the support of both USC and the City of Pasadena in enabling Richard and me to preserve and continue sharing this blessed spiritual environment and its activities even beyond our life on this planet, we are exceedingly grateful.

To psychologist Gerald Davison, PhD, who served as interim Dean of the USC School of Architecture during the incipient discussion of our giving our home to that institution and to which he lent his esteemed advice and positive response, our gratitude forever.

To Randell Makinson, Director Emeritus of Charles and Henry Greene's masterpiece, the 1908 Gamble House/USC, who educated me decades ago in my understanding that Buff & Hensman were really the Greene and Greene of the second half of the twentieth century, my respect and devotion always.

To Miller Yee Fong – Don Hensman's personal recommendation as the ideal artist to introduce readers to Arroyo del Rey visually – a million bouquets for both illustrating and designing this book. And more bouquets for Bryan Bosworth, principal, BBcreative, Miller's personal pick for bringing to these pages the necessary technical and visual expertise.

To Ann Gray, founder/publisher of Balcony Press and its highly regarded books on architecture, my deep appreciation for your help and sensitive guidance of my first purely inspirational manuscript. To author/artist/educator Elizabeth Gill Lui, my gratitude for your incomparable care in reviewing this manuscript. To the discriminating Jetty Fong and wordsmith Sally Sturdy Beaudette, thank you from the bottom of my heart for your exquisitely fine suggestions during the final stages of producing this book.

Of course, my many blessings began with my supportive and inspirational parents Romus and Anne Soucek for being at my side always and for financially supporting the future maintenance endowment for The King Center/USC. My life and whatever I create have also been blessed by the unending inspiration of my brother, Philip Merrill Soucek, CDR, U.S. Navy, 1941-1979, and my grandparents John and Frances Stejskal Soucek, and Estelle Merrill Boyce and Dr. William Alexander Boyce.

And every day those blessings continue and multiply with having as my husband Richard King, mentor to so many about not only international understanding but also the riches of the heart.

Finally, a million hugs to our dog Gypsy, ever present at our side, expressing Love sunup to sundown – and then some!

ABOUT THE ILLUSTRATOR & BOOK DESIGNER

Miller Yee Fong is one of those people who seemed to be born an artist and whose talent has shaped his path throughout his life and career. He grew up in his family's Los Angeles-based furniture business, Fong Brothers Company (formerly Tropi-Cal), following his father Danny Ho Fong in designing contemporary rattan furniture known for its artistry, detail and fresh perspective. The award-winning furniture by both father and son has been published and exhibited widely, including numerous museums (two Danny Ho Fong designs are in the permanent collection of the Museum of Modern Art, New York). In addition, Miller Fong has been a practicing architect since graduating with honors in 1964 from the University of Southern California School of Architecture, and has designed homes coveted by friends and family in Southern California and Hawaii. It is at USC's School of Architecture where, in his class "Architect's Sketchbook," Fong teaches the fine art of sketching, which to him is an innate natural gift but which to most architects in this digital world has become an almost lost skill.

Fong and his wife Jetty reside in Pasadena, California, and their worldwide travels are captured in his series of coveted sketchbooks, as are the events in the lives of the Fongs' friends and family – which includes two daughters, their husbands and their six grandchildren.

ABOUT THE AUTHOR

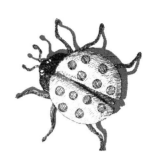

Carol Soucek King, MFA, PhD, has always believed that the only aspect of our life on earth worth expressing is its spiritual nature. This is what she has hoped to emphasize through her community involvement, her ongoing support of international cultural exchange, and through her professional activities – actress, teacher, drama critic, newspaper writer and editor, magazine editor, and author of twelve books on the design of homes and gardens throughout the world. She lives in Pasadena, California, with her husband Richard King and it is there where in 1996 she founded The Salon on the Spiritually Creative Life. The Salon is usually held in their home which the Kings built with architects Conrad Buff III, FAIA, and Don Hensman, FAIA. Named "Arroyo del Rey," their home has been designated a Historic Monument by the City of Pasadena. In the future, it will become The Carol Soucek King and Richard King Center for Architecture, Arts and the Humanities/ School of Architecture, University of Southern California.

Dr. King graduated from Marlborough School, received a Bachelor of Arts degree in English literature from the University of Southern California, a Master of Fine Arts in Drama from Yale University, and a Doctor of Philosophy in Communications from USC. She also completed a summer course in English literature at Cambridge University, England.

ABOUT THE TYPE

Chris Costello, a designer and calligrapher as well as typographer, created Papyrus in 1982 by hand, drafting the font on textured paper with a calligraphy pen over a six month period; the lettering was drawn to emulate what the designer felt the English language would have looked like, had it been written on papyrus 2000 years ago. The Letraset foundry published the type, producing as a series of transferable lettering sheets otherwise known as "presstype." Subsequently the font was digitized and the rights sold to ITC (later Monotype).

Papyrus' unique appeal includes its use of high horizontal strokes, rough edges and sweeping curves – a merging of Roman typography with calligraphy. Papyrus continues to be popular in design and desktop publishing both commercially and privately; the Elsner+Flake company has produced a Papyrus EF™ font family variation, featuring multiple new swash additions and lettering changes.*

*Source: www.fonts.com

Made in the USA
Charleston, SC
17 November 2012